The Navigator

By Christopher Register

Contents

The Navigator

Introduction

I'd say the year was 1990...yeah, that sounds about right. The universe, god, the source—whatever one likes to call the higher power at play—was trying to teach me something. Unfortunately, at that time, I wasn't aware of what life was about, not at all. I was just a young kid. I knew nothing about how life worked and what the heck I was even doing here. I had very little chances of picking up on the small but powerful secrets that had probably been placed in front of me since the day of my birth—I was too busy being fascinated and soaking up the beauty that was all around me.

But then again, I was only eight years old, and I was just following in the path of my elders. Never did I have thoughts like "Why I was here?" or "What's this world about?" I was just downloading what society, my parents, and my teachers were telling me. I was under their guidance and felt that they knew what was best for me.

If only I had been wise enough to pick up on things faster though. Then I would not have been saying things like "I wish I would have done this differently" or that differently later in life. If only I had a manual about how to operate life.

There I was, in east central Florida. The sun was out, the sky was bright blue, and there was barely a cloud in the sky...yet I was indoors sitting in a classroom, either staring at a chalkboard or what an overhead projector was projecting. I was probably learning something—or better said, I was probably *trying* to learn something like basic math or proper spelling along with the other students. I rarely paid attention in class though as I thought most of the subjects were kind of boring to me.

But luckily for me, during this particular moment, we got to have one of our daily breaks. Whenever we did, our teacher, Mrs. Ryan, would ask us all to line up single-file line in front of the classroom door. As the line started to form, one could probably find me in one or two places: either at the front because I liked to be first and feel like the leader (go figure) or next to wherever a cute girl was standing (go figure again).

At our age, lining up was always delayed a bit since our behavior could easily get out of hand. Once our teacher was able to get us to be orderly, she would escort us to the playground out in the large field for recess. That day, as always, we continued following our teacher out the door, down the sidewalk, and through the grass toward the playground. As we approached the playground, we just continued on, heading to some open grass. That was something we had been doing since the start of the school year. The administrators had given our class a job to do, and prior to our recess break, our teacher made sure we did just that. I guess the school wanted to spruce up the scenery a bit, so they gave us an oak tree to plant and then maintain. Our class was in charge of that tree throughout the year to provide it with the attention it needed to grow. It was our job to make sure that we took care of it every day to help bring it to life and eventually fully mature.

Not a day went by that we didn't check on the tree and make sure it was getting what it needed. I was still a student at that school for the next several years, so I was able to watch our tree continue to grow. By the time I left, the tree was strong enough to maintain itself on it its own. As I think about that tree today, I can now see that it kind of thanked us in a way— after what we did for it, it gave us something back such as great beauty and lots of shade. It even provided housing for animals like birds and squirrels and oxygen for humanity. In essence, the tree had actually established its own purpose in life. Incredible. So the question is, could it also really be that easy to establish a purpose in life such as that tree?

Now that I think about it today—what my class and I did with that tree is an example of what I feel many living beings on earth can accomplish, such as you and I. All of us I feel can apply this approach to any area of our life. If we give our energy and our attention to the things we want so dearly and we continue to give them attention day in and day out, we will be rewarded with a wonderful result, and even more so, possibly a purpose. It really is that simple. Now, I don't expect many people to automatically share this belief of mine that I now have, and there are some things one needs to zone in on first before getting started. From what I know the majority of people need more than just words to believe in something— they usually need to see a result or some sort of proof or experience something themselves to believe it.

But what I can do is actually encourage one to start thinking about that tree as an example and many other things I'm going to talk about in this book. The majority of what I've written is based not on just my discoveries, but on my experiences and results in life. For instance, I'm now aware of a few of the laws that govern this planet, more specifically the law of balance. That's something I've come to recognize that's at play all around me, which earlier in life I had no idea. It may seem a bit early to mention this topic, but now that I've shared it, allow me to explain what I mean.

Think about the time and effort my class and I gave to the tree right. Slowly, day by day, the tree gave us results; little by little, the tree matched our efforts. We caused a give-to-get situation to occur by our actions and what we provided. The tree grew as a direct result of our actions. We had filled up one side of the scale, and the tree filled up the other side.

The law of balance had come into play. When you give something attention, you'll receive that same level of attention back, whether it's something easy or something difficult. (More on that later.) The law of balance is just one aspect of life that seems obvious to me today, yet still seems to be hidden from many: if you give something attention, it will give *you* attention. Which I suppose this is similar to Sir Isaac Newton's Third Law, which states that for every action, there is an equal and opposite reaction. But having this understanding and belief is just a small piece of the puzzle, as far as knowledge that one can use as a tool in the game of life.

None of us have ever received a handbook or instructions on how to operate life. There was no manual given. All most of us were told by everyone around us was that we needed to go to college and then in turn we'd make good money. If one didn't do that then it was a bad thing. I know that's all that really got passed on to me. I could, as well as others have used a bit more input to say the least—we *all* could use more.

Well, I'm now 36 years old, and what you're about to read about is life as I know it...and how I am playing it.

We All Want One Thing

I have come to realize that what the majority of us think we want from life is incorrect—it's just smoke and mirrors. What we really want goes deeper than just exotic cars, waterfront mansions, yachts, private jets, millions of dollars in the bank, a super attractive woman or man by our side, luxury fashion accessories, traveling, partying with celebrities, etc. I mean, yes, those all sound nice, but even if one has those things, we can still feel very unfulfilled in life and are likely searching for more meaning. It's easy for our minds to get clouded when we focus only on things like having more social status or obtaining tangible items. We see that as "having the good life," and we think we would be happy if we could get it. But that's a very one-dimensional view of what "the good life" is and what the life we *truly* want is all about. Unfortunately, most people are unaware that their goal then becomes the pursuit for what will allow them to obtain what they perceive as needing to have:

Money.

If money was what truly made us happy in life, then why would people with plenty of it and social status seek help from the ever-popular self-help guru Tony Robbins? Well, I think it's clear as they're still unsatisfied with their lives. If you don't know who Tony is, through his seminars and books, he has educated many people on how to obtain a meaningful life. He has helped many people and some being billionaires. As I write this, I can't help but think of a conversation I had with a good friend of mine the other day. He owns his own business and has been doing very well for himself. Recently, I ran into him and his wife at a mutual gathering. We greeted each other as always and then started the small talk—you know, how's life, how's your business going, that sort of thing. Once I went with the "How's life?" question, that seemed to be a trigger for him. Immediately, he began to vent. I could tell that he was stressed-out and just frustrated with his position in life. Here's what he said:

"Chris, I'm over this fancy life. At first, it's great having all these nice things, but what does it really mean? It doesn't really matter! I'm a slave to these things I've acquired, and I'm not really enjoying life. It's just not fun anymore. All I do is work to make more money. Yes, I have nice things, but for what? To impress other people and keep up with the Joneses. My wife and I are about to sell everything and minimalize our life to start enjoying ourselves more. I have three cars right now, and I don't need that."

At the time, my friend knew how I was playing my life. The moment he was having was the same moment I had had not too long ago. I was making great money—especially for my age—and I had some of "the finer things in life." But what I *didn't* have was time, because I was constantly having to renew vehicle tags, get insurance, maintain my things, etc. And that vicious cycle I'd fallen into continued as I kept working more to keep making more money so that I'd continue to have those things and acquire new ones. I felt flat inside; I became aware that I was caught in a cycle and was not really fulfilled at all by it. That's when I decided to go backwards in order to go forward again in life. I liquidated all of my cars, furniture, ATVs, and even my house. Yes, I got rid of my own home. (In case you were wondering, I have no dependents.) I did this to restructure my life because I wanted to have another crack at my life. This time around, I knew that

I would have more knowledge and life lessons under my belt... I wanted to play my life better.

My friend and his wife were doing the same thing. Their end goal might have been different, but all of us ultimately went down the same path and discovered the same thing: unfulfillment.

I want you to know that fulfillment isn't about how much money you can make. The person with the most money or things isn't guaranteed a satisfying life (even though the less fortunate may perceive that they are living a fabulous life). As I've said, the majority of what we're supposed to want in life is smoke and mirrors. It's simply inaccurate. Now, money will play a part in achieving "the good life," yes. I don't mean to say that money doesn't matter at all, I'm just saying that we should not put money on a pedestal. It shouldn't be our main focus—if/when it is, it clouds our mind and prevents us from focusing on other important areas of life.

If I were to only tell you how to achieve money and things in life, I'd be failing you, because there's a huge chance you would still be unfulfilled and unhappy. I would have failed to share what life is really about and give you knowledge on how to navigate it best, which is the reason of this book.

Now it's time to change the tone slightly just for a bit. I hate to say this, but I believe that often, being helpful means being brutally honest. Here it is: everyone—you, me, everyone else—in this world is selfish. I'm sorry if that comes off as harsh or judgmental, but it's true. Every single person in this world is selfish—they just don't fully realize it. That's because everything we do in life is all for one reason and one reason only:

We all just want to "feel good." I'm going to repeat that.

All everyone is trying to do is just *make themselves feel good.*

That may sound pretty silly and basic at first, but once one starts to think about what drives them through life, it all leads back to just that: wanting to feel good. I once thought that the reason I bought someone a gift or gave them a shoulder to cry on was unselfish, which it does appear to be on the surface. But deep down, all of us operate in such a manner because it ultimately makes us personally feel good. I felt it was the right thing to do, so by doing that, I felt good for doing it. We want people in our lives because they make us feel good. (Which in turn is why we don't want to lose them.) We want that car or that fancy house because it makes us feel good. I could go on and on about all of the little things in life and why we do what we do, but it will always go back to one thing: making ourselves feel good.

But enough of that for now—I'll be sharing much more about our motives and how we can use those revelations to craft better lives for ourselves. The whole objective of this book is to pass along my discoveries and insights to try and help others improve their lives. I'd love for everyone to have a better direction and plan to navigate life to its fullest. The mainstream messages provided to the humanity don't seem to be helping us much. I want others to win, and right now, it seems the majority of us are simply not.

At the end of the day, people will do one of two things: they will either make an effort to go after everything they want in life, or they will adopt a poor mindset and complain that life sucks. That's because some of us have received poor guidance and just aren't feeling good about ourselves or about our lives. It's really that simple. A negative mindset doesn't come about because life sucks, it comes about because that person didn't respond properly to life. They didn't understand what's happening on the playing field. They didn't know how to operate this so-called "game" of life.

I like to call it a game because life is very similar to many video games we play today. Slight tangent here: I anticipate that the gaming industry will get even bigger and that virtual reality will spike to a level where just about every household gets involved. That's because humans want to feel good, and if the world we live in today doesn't provide us with ways to feel good, then humans will naturally drift to places that do. That's why so many people play video games—the games allow us to live in a different world where we can be who we want to be and achieve what we want to achieve. When we lose in the virtual world, we don't feel that loss as much, because our subconscious knows we can just try again. Either way, virtual worlds provide us with good feelings, feelings that are easier to achieve than what many of us are getting in actuality. While I don't think this is an overall good thing, I just can understand why people will want to immerse themselves in virtual worlds and why virtual reality will *be* our reality one day. People will want to check out from their real lives—lives that might not be as fruitful—to get a high in their digital life.

But the truth is that *this* life, this *real life* outside of the virtual world, can be just as successful as a video game, yet 95% of the population doesn't know how to make that happen. We aren't being guided or cared for properly—for one thing, we allow our kids to consume food that damages how our brains work and how we feel. And that's just the tip of the iceberg! Today, the majority of us—especially the up-and-coming generations—are buried in our phones. The next step will be probably going all the way into the digital world.

Before I continue, I want to stop and call myself out on something. Considering that I've said that everyone is selfish, am I being selfish right now? Am I being selfish by writing this book?

The honest answer is yes, absolutely. I'm only writing this book because my creator built me to get a "feel good" sensation when I help other humans. So yes, I'm being selfish by helping others, because ultimately, helping others helps *me* feel better about what I'm doing with my life. It gives me meaning and maybe even a sense of purpose.

Sounds a little crazy, but maybe it's also a nice thing, right? Especially when we are making a positive impact on others to give that positive impact on ourselves. When did "selfish" become such a bad word? After all, when we're giving to others in the process, the law of balance is taking place. Seems like a fair deal, a balanced deal. It's like in that Hollywood film about Jerry Maguire (the movie with Tom Cruise and Cuba Gooding, Jr.) when Maguire says to Rod Tidwell, "Help *me* help *you.*" Well, that's give to get, that's balance. But we will talk more about that later.

I think it's time to look at things a little deeper so that we can get you better equipped to level up as a person. Because—and pardon my language here—I know damn well that no one else is really truly trying to help you. As I look around, I see that most people are wandering around cluelessly, living a

Level 5 feel-good life when they could be doing better. We all deserve more.

And what do I mean by a "Level 5 feel-good life"? Let's say we put ten people on a beach. Each has a chair, an umbrella, and a drink of their choice. All are facing the ocean, feeling the beautiful breeze and the energizing sunlight.

Guess what? All ten people will feel differently. One may still be depressed, another may feel so-so, and others may feel amazing. Why? Yes, we all are created differently, but is the person who feels amazing doing something right and the rest of us aren't? Out of those ten people, let's say that person is probably living at least a Level 7 feel-good whether they're on the beach or not. Life is about more than just one simple aspect. (In this case, simply where you are.) Life is about focusing on many aspects to give yourself balance which that person may be doing whether they're aware or not.

The first aspect we'll look at is the four main categories or pillars in life. If we take the time to think about the four categories, we'll see they give us this sense of balance and a sense of completion, as if we are checking off everything to a person's life. If we learn to fill up these categories for ourselves, we can most likely achieve mastery of the game of life. I personally strive to attain a Level 7 or higher in each of the pillars.

Below is a chart to give you a visual of the four categories I'm talking about:

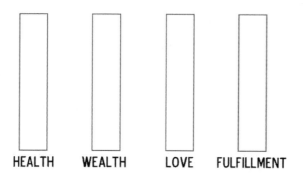

THE FOUR CATEGORIES OF YOUR LIFE

HEALTH   WEALTH   LOVE   FULFILLMENT

So here's how this works: one should first, honestly grade themselves from 1 to 10 in each of the pillars above, then add them up and divide by four. That number will tell a person what kind of life they're living.

As an example, I will give you a snapshot of my life at the moment. I'd say my health is 7, my wealth is 8, my love and relationships is a 2, and my fulfillment is an 8. My overall result is 6.25, which isn't bad. I know what area I lack in and I know what exactly to do. I'm that close to creating a balanced life for myself, and I must admit that it feels pretty great. Which is what I want for everyone else to feel, great, too, and enjoy a life they are blessed to have.

You see, the secret to living the good life isn't just about the "finer things in life." Sure, they help when it comes to the wealth column and they play a factor in our overall happiness, but in order to achieve the kind of good life we all truly want, then the other columns must be filled up, too. We must give all of them attention and strive to push each one of them to be above a 7. I think that's a fair goal. Anything over 7 is great; anything near 10 would be considered close to mastery.

Navigation Knowledge

The ultimate goal for everyone is to just feel good, and whoever is able to do that—whoever can achieve the highest level in all four columns—is winning at life. A wise approach is to focus on giving attention to each of the four categories so that they can fill up. Doing so will help one achieve a balanced life, which will result in great fulfillment.

Our Health Pillar

The very first thing in life that one should fully understand is how to be healthy. I know this might seem like a boring topic, but it is the most important one. Babies and toddlers can't wrap their heads around this, but eventually, we get to an age where we can comprehend things more clearly. Whether through school lessons or parental guidance, that's when how to be healthy should be explained to us in detail. We need to know this well before we set sail in life. We don't necessarily need to know how every cell in the body functions, but we do need to know what the body should run on, and we should know about the serious repercussions of the kinds of diseases we could wind up with if we choose not to follow a path of health. Honestly, we should not focus on anything else until we understand the body we have been given.

Understanding our bodies allows us to experience our ultimate goal in life: feeling good. We should all be educated that having a healthy body allows us to feel the positive emotions in life. That's something worth repeating: health should be our #1 focus, because a healthy body gives us the good feelings we're all striving for. If we don't treat our bodies properly, we won't have our innate human ability to feel good, and if we can't get those feel-good vibes, then our interests and goals in life become less desirable. What would one be doing right now if they had lost the ability to feel good? Well they would probably be desperately trying to do the things they used to do that made them feel good, trying to get back that high in life they once had. Unfortunately, a lot of people are going through this right now, because they have lost that feel good factor in life. This is something I want to prevent from happening to others out there.

The majority of us were never truly taught why our health is so important. This lack of awareness can be detrimental to living a moderately comfortable life, let alone a happy one. Most of us take our health for granted until *BOOM!* something shifts. A person's mood can change for the worse, and they can start to very easily project negativity into the world. That's when they start behaving outside of their own true self, looking for ways to cope because they've lost their ability to feel good. Often, this is a slow trend that the person doesn't recognize, and unfortunately, they may turn to things such as drugs and alcohol for relief. Of course, that doesn't help in the long run. Worse yet, as more time goes on, chronic disease can start setting in. This has become a common occurrence based on my observation today.

This entire process unfortunately boils down to the general lack of knowledge of how to be healthy, leading to us misunderstanding and mistreating our bodies. It becomes a domino effect, a slow process that starts to nudge us toward a less motivated and unhealthy kind of living, a life that has really just lost its zest, a life that can lead to relying on substances or medicines to try to make ourselves feel good. But that's just a quick temporary fix for a compromised body—while medicine can help, it can't permanently solve the problem when the root is the person self-inflicting unhealthy lifestyle. Or we may resort to illegal substances instead, creating a potential addiction and a negative cycle that repeats itself again and again.

Let's take a moment to think about this state of un-health. We can see that everyone wants the same thing in life right: to just feel good in a natural way. Two key factors to making sure that happens is having are a proper dietary intake and also a clean environment. Both play a role as they are the sources that affect our system internally.

I'm sure many have heard this before, but I'd like to reference it here: if we don't have our health, then what do we have? Well, we have nothing. Without our health, we're done. All of our worries and wants vanish and no longer hold any weight in our life. The car we've enjoyed driving, the goals we were pursuing, the sport we loved to play, the person we wanted to become, the song or book we wanted to write... All of these things are no longer a part of our lives if we don't remain in good health.

If we look at the diagram below, we can see that health is at the core of life.

If our health deteriorates, it will affect our connection with everything in life, including the people we love dearly. We will unfortunately miss out on the beauty that's in store for us. While we don't need to understand the body's complex biological processes to be able to care for ourselves, we should understand what can damage our bodies. Let's look a little deeper at what we're putting into our body and how that's related to the possibility of losing our ability to feel good.

Losing the Ability to Feel Good

Many things can become health issues that can contribute to us losing our ability to feel good. One of the main things is that there is a connection between the gut and the brain. It might sound far-fetched to many, but the latest discovery is that the gut is connected to the brain and that 90% of serotonin is produced in the gut.

What is serotonin and why is it important? Serotonin (or 5-hydroxytryptamine) is a monoamine neurotransmitter, although some claim that it's a hormone instead. But researchers do agree that serotonin contributes to feelings of well-being and happiness. Many of us may have seen commercials for SSRIs. (Which are targeting humans main goal right? to feel good.) That stands for Selective Serotonin Re-uptake Inhibitors, and they're marketed as a drug that helps alleviate depression and anxiety. SSRIs are commonly used drugs today. Without going into exact numbers, many studies say that 1 in 6 or even 1 in 8 people over the age of 12 are taking SSRIs, often because of genetic factors. Genetics being the reason for these issues strikes me as silly—in my opinion, as our individual genetics to me are related to how much pollution a person can handle before symptoms arise or if a particular food or substance is even tolerable.

I can explain a little more in detail. For example, just because John can eat wheat and not feel bad doesn't mean that Debbie will be able to—she might have a confirmed case of celiac disease and wheat might make her feel terrible. That's genetics. (Although just because John doesn't feel bad when he eats wheat, that doesn't mean that the wheat isn't harming him and that it's okay for him to consume wheat. He could still have celiac disease and not know it because he's asymptomatic.) In Debbie's case, if she addresses the root cause—that is, if she removes wheat from her diet—the problem is resolved. Unfortunately, in the US, if Debbie were to see a doctor complaining of stomach issues, she'd probably be given prescriptions for relief of her symptoms without much thought toward what the root cause might be. In turn this allows for even more things in the body to go wrong as the main source never gets resolved. More prescriptions get added to the person's list as time goes on due to new symptoms arises from the unresolved source. Rather than just always chalking our problems up to genetics, we need to also think about what we're designed to run on. This is an important point to consider, especially in our current environment.

What we eat day in and day out is highly likely the leading cause of symptoms and the collective deterioration of humanity's health. It's also key to remember that things consumed in moderation are less likely to be a problem versus things we consume on a regular basis, so please keep that in mind. If someone ate at McDonald's just once a month or enjoyed a soda just once a month, their body would be able to deal with the poor dietary choice more easily. The issue is when someone constantly consumes low-quality food or anything not good on a regular basis. *That's* when we start to jeopardize our health. The wide gaps of moderation are fine, as long as it doesn't become a habit. Which now brings me to something I'd like to share.

Have you ever seen the movie *Back to the Future Part II* with Doc Brown and Marty McFly? (Depending on your age, you probably have—it's a classic.) There's a scene in the movie that reminds me of the human conditioning today. It's the part where Doc Brown pulls up at Marty's house and wants Marty to come back to the future. And Doc Brown's flying time machine needs fuel, so he goes through Marty's garbage can outside, grabbing old trash and throwing it into the fuel tank because his time-traveling vehicle can run on it. I see this part of the movie as a parallel to what most Americans are doing to themselves: our bodies cannot efficiently run on the processed foods, and we're not going to adapt to this diet. Instead, what most of us eat will cause our bodies to slowly deteriorate until eventually disease sets in. And let's think about the word *disease* for a moment. It means that the body is no longer at ease—it's at dis-ease.

Here's something else that's kind of baffling when we stop and think about it. It seems that the majority of people today take better care of their cars than their own bodies. They make sure those beautiful cars they own are kept all nice and pretty—clean on the outside and clean on the inside. They make sure to change the oil on time, and they always, always put only gas in the tank and nothing else. We take care of our cars this way because we know that not doing so can lead to problems, such as breakdowns and the car not starting at all. We wouldn't want our cars to break down, no. We have spent so much money to purchase them. Hmm...there's that putting-money-on-the-pedestal thing again. It's funny that for many of us, our car—something that depreciates in value day by day—gets more attention than our body. It seems the average person understands how their car works better than they understand how their own body works.

When I think about what our bodies do for us, it's pretty amazing. We can beat the crap out of it, and it just copes with the problem. It doesn't always alert us immediately when something is wrong. You know what it does with problem instead? It deals with it. Yes, our bodies deal with the constant punishment we give them, because most of us were never truly taught what the body was designed to run on. And we're never taught what we should—need to—avoid, either. Its constantly under battle and unaware by the person until symptoms show up.

If we observe animals in the wild that have not been influenced by humans, we notice that they consume what they were designed to consume. The result is a fully functional system. Obviously, there are exceptions—sometimes genetics do go awry—but this isn't generally the case for wild animals like monkeys, tigers, rhinos, and whales. Their environment and food source isn't being altered. But if we look at domesticated animals, like farm animals and pets, we notice that they experience diseases like tumors and skin problems just like we do. This is because their food source which is artificially created by humans is their diet. Imagine if also we altered the food intake and environment in the wild. Artificial food, exhaust fumes etc. The results will not be good, just as a majority of ours aren't. We all are natural beings and it seems wise to consume also what is natural, not artificial.

Many people are focused on having a nice car or other tangible items that provide a short-term high in life. But the most important thing that allows people to have good feelings—the body—is taken for granted. It's usually only when a person finally realizes that they are losing their health that they even try to treat their body the way it should be treated. Unfortunately, most of us must feel some pain or go through some loss in order to make changes.

I could go on and on about how important this health pillar is and what affects it, like external factors that are altering our environment. If you would like to know more, I recommend checking out my book *See the Cube and Not the Square,* in which I go over these pillars in more detail. I am only reviewing them briefly here because understanding the four pillars is an essential part of being a good navigator of life.

Below are some of my healthy lifestyle habits. Some may seem like they're a bit much to the average person, but my health is my #1 priority.

- I consume prebiotics and probiotics daily to help feed good bacteria in the gut.

- Chicken bone broth is essential in my diet for healing the gut and absorbing collagen.

- I take good-quality supplements of vitamins A, B, C, and D, and B12 daily. I also take coconut oil, iodine, selenium, l-glutamine, magnesium, and fish oil, to name just a few.

- Occasionally, I detox with chlorella, spirulina, and milk thistle.

- Eating fast food is not a routine for me. I cook a lot and make wise selections when I do eat out.

- My diet is a balanced one, consisting of high-protein foods, low- and medium-carb foods, medium-fat foods, and foods with low or medium amounts of sodium.

- Some of my favorite foods and beverages are: chicken, beef, turkey, zucchini, squash, sweet potatoes, broccoli, plain Greek yogurt, strawberries, apples, raspberries, walnuts, almonds, water, and green tea. In moderation, I do treat myself to foods like pizza and tacos from time to time. I do go out and enjoy myself at social settings that include alcohol, but not frequently.

- I exercise for a minimum of an hour at least three times a week.

- I limit my Wi-Fi exposure and do not have it in my home—I only have hardwired devices. Cellular I do have but sleep with my devices on airplane mode.

Navigation Knowledge

You are what you eat. If you put crap in, you will eventually feel like crap. If you put good stuff in, you'll feel good. Remember, your body often doesn't alert you of problems right away—it just deals with them. Don't let mainstream commercial food options suck you into the system and slowly alter your body and your mind. Recognize what's good for your health and find foods that support your goals. Commercial food manufacturers don't care about your health, just your money. *That's* what's at the top of their list.

Our Wealth Pillar

Wealth can be defined in many different ways, but here we will talk about the most popular form of wealth, which is money. Money drives the decisions and actions of many people, often and unfortunately for the wrong reasons. Just as many people do not understand their own bodies, they also might not understand why money has such an effect on them. In the world we live in, we need money to survive comfortably. If we don't make enough money, we end up not being able to pay for three main necessities I feel we need in life. (More about those three in a minute.) For the majority of us, the three necessities should be easy to attain and maintain with very little struggle. The problem is that many of us have not learned financial intelligence; we seem to just live in the moment and make purchases based on our emotions, and not logic. Most of the time, we are living beyond our means. This appears to go for the bulk of the world.

So what are the three main necessities? Well, we definitely need water and food in order for our bodies to function. This fact supports the idea that health is our #1 priority. The second necessity is shelter, a place where we are protected from dangerous weather and where we have a comfortable place to rest so that our wonderful bodies can heal themselves. The third necessity is clothing. Depending on where we live and the season, we need different kinds of clothing for comfort and protection from the weather. Transportation could be considered a fourth necessity, but it's borderline because we have our own two feet that enable us to get around. That said, transportation does make it easy for us to get to our destinations, and depending on where people live, may not require a big purchase. Transportation includes taking a cab, bus, or train; riding a bicycle or a scooter; or driving a car.

If we consider the three undisputed necessities that allow us to live (and potentially include transportation as the fourth necessity), how much wealth is really required to have these things? The main expense, which is never-ending and always shifting, is for food and water, although there are ways to lessen some of those costs—for example, you can produce your own food, however that's difficult to do for the majority of people today.

Do we know why many people are having a hard time living comfortably? Our clothing can be purchased affordably and doesn't need to be a long-term expense in our life. A vehicle doesn't necessarily require a large monthly payment. And shelter, which is the biggest expense for most people, can eventually become a nonrevolving expense outside of utilities and taxes

The reason most of us are not living comfortably is because we have not acquired financial intelligence, which was not taught early on—it must be eventually learned. Poor money management skills result from a lack of education about finances. How to prioritize and manage money properly is how one develops financial intelligence. Go ahead and add to the lack of financial intelligence a unhealthy body that houses an unhealthy mind, and this adds to the problem of one properly managing money to pay for their necessities and become financially successful. Once again, our #1 priority should be our health, and if we aren't healthy, our lives are affected at a level many people might not even be aware of like interrupting financial success

As I slowly try to connect these dots, I hope you'll see that it's time to move forward in a new direction. Before thinking about attaining great wealth, be sure to take care of your health. Consuming low-quality foods makes people feel depressed, and then they try to find relief by eating more low-quality foods or buying tangible items in an attempt to curb their lack of fulfillment, that feel good. This poisonous cycle puts people in a bad financial situation: they aren't managing their money properly, and they're spending money on products they don't really need and quite possibly can't even afford. These items usually are not necessities, and current average incomes aren't usually enough to support purchasing these non-necessities. All of this means that the process of making big gains in the wealth column becomes disrupted and much harder for us to achieve.

Lack of Motivation

The main thing that prevents people from going out and achieving their goal of great wealth is a lack of motivation and drive. Poor health can easily be a contributing factor to this— as I've said previously, everything is interconnected. A good friend of mine once asked me the million-dollar question...or make that the billion-dollar question, because that's what it should be worth today. The question is: how do you get someone who isn't motivated to be motivated? At that time, I really didn't have the complete answer. A few months later, though, as I was being interviewed by the host of a radio podcast, the host asked me the same question. This time, I felt had a better response.

Outside of poor health being a big factor behind feeling demotivated, finding motivation really starts with doing the following. My suggestion to him probably seemed quite strange at first. I told him that everyone should go lock themselves in a room (Obviously still being able to exit) with no electronic devices, a quiet place where they can tap into great thoughts.

They should then ask themselves what are probably the three most important questions in a person's life which are the following:

· Who am I?

· What do I want?

· Why do I want that?

This is where everything starts; a person being able to answer these questions are why some people might be motivated and while others are simply not. Some people may not have answered the first question, but they've identified the second question—what they want—through their own thoughts or perhaps by observing others. Usually, money is in the equation, along with some tangible items they find appealing. Now, I can easily answer these questions myself, but only because I wanted more from life so I started thinking a lot. Once I had answered the three, I turned inward some more and started to learn about myself. So likewise, one must also be able to answer these questions for themselves as well. I'll talk about a fourth important question later. (It doesn't come into effect until you can answer the first three.)

For some people, seeing the success of others makes them question their own lives and in turn helps them answer what they want. I say this because that's what happened to me when I was around 19 years old. At the time, I was working at a warehouse, collecting orders and shipping packages for cellular accessory products. Each month, franchisee business owners would stop by, and when they stopped by, they *stopped by*. I can still remember watching them pull up in their Ferraris and Lotuses. Do you think my mind got clouded quickly with money and tangible items? It sure did! But things have changed for me since then as I see things differently.

However, that was when I started to question myself and take a good look at what those business owners had figured out. That's what kicked things into gear for me and got me thinking...which then gave me a *want* in life. I answered the second question which I turned into a goal.

And BOOM! Just like that, I was motivated. I wanted to be like those franchise owners! I wanted to be making tons of money and driving fancy cars.

Goals give us something to go after in life—when we wake up in the morning, we are looking forward to achieving that goal. We are motivated. Each and every day, progress is made, and like the great motivational speaker Tony Robbins says, progress equals happiness. This statement goes hand-in-hand with another statement: life is all about the journey. The journey is what keeps us alive and makes us feel good. If someone's progress is making them happy in life and we know they ultimately want to feel good, then they'd be motivated to take even more action as it feels good, right? It's such a win win and a great motivator to someone. But prior to making that progress we all need to at least answer the second question to give ourselves something to make progress on, something to go after.

Reached a Goal

Achieving an end result is rewarding, yes, but it can also be depressing, because then we ask ourselves another important question: What do I do next?

This often happens when people retire. They lose that feeling of being valued or needed; they feel as if they no longer have a place in the world. This can happen if a person isn't following their passion or purpose which I will discuss later. In extreme cases, they may feel so aimless that they slip into depression when a goal is reach, which can be retirement. However, the positive side when we reach the end of a tough journey, we look back through our memories, we start to feel the beauty reaching that goal. Not because of the goal itself, but because we cannot believe what we have accomplished along the way. The obstacles we once thought were insurmountable we now see as simply having been stepping stones. Having many goals and passionate ones at that typically doesn't result in one stopping after one goal is reached. There really is no retiring, instead the person actually feels like they're *living* because passion and purpose are guiding them.

Earl Nightingale has a great audiobook in which he discusses why some people are more successful than others. The simple answer is that successful people have *goals*. If you want to fill up your wealth column, then you must have goals. To create goals, ask yourself the three questions I mentioned earlier, and more specifically the second one. Your answers will help you get there.

The other day, I wrote this message to myself on my dry-erase board:

"People need goals to keep them alive. Having no goals will lead to an unfulfilling life."

If I didn't have anything to go after in life, for example, what would I be doing? I definitely don't want to use the time I've been given to just enjoy the creations of other people—I would like to leave something behind for them, too. I want to try to make the world a better place while I am here. Maybe that's something one thinks about as well. Almost every tangible thing around us that helps make up life was created by someone no different than you or I. The thing that we know the creators had was a goal. Not only did they have a goal, they had a passion in life, one that held meaning for them. Yes, while many of these creators also made lots of money, attaining wealth wasn't the main driver for them.

Deep down, we all want to do something great and contribute to our world, but not all of us know where to start. Many people have never even answered the first question, the question of "Who am I?" because they've never even thought about it.

A business adviser I followed named Tai Lopez once shared something with me. He said that there are three types of people in this world:

"People who make things happen
People who watch things happen
People who wonder what happened."

The first two are fine, he stated. However, he pointed out that you don't ever want to be the person who wonders what happened.

Will Money Make Us Happy?

I talked about this previously, but since we are still in the wealth column, I felt I should address this concept again here. I feel we are all creators; we want to create and do great things. However, the majority of us are unaware and are simply conforming to what others around us are doing. We all have great gifts and talents we haven't tapped into yet...and tragically, most likely, we never will. Most people do not yet have a full mind-body connection because of the system we live in and its effects on us. Many people make poor decisions on a daily basis because many people lack an understanding of life and themselves.

All of this happens because most of us are driven by one major impetus: chasing the money. And the reason why we chase the money is just for one reason: to buy things, mostly things that other people create. I must say that it's better to be on the side of creating things than buying things. If you want to increase your wealth, then tap into your creativity and make things happen. It's best not to be on the other end wondering what happened. Being on the "creator" end can mean being a seller, whereas not creating means you're always a buyer. Creators are giving themselves more of a chance of becoming wealthy than the buyers are. Creators have goals and passions; buyers may very well not. And I feel the need to point out that a passion I speak about is much more than an interest—it's more like a love.

The person without passions or goals is the one who is most likely conforming to the mainstream culture. That person is also probably not being an independent thinker. (More on that later.) Most people say that if they get a certain item (e.g., a car, a house, a new TV), then they will be happy. Or better said, they *think* they will be happy, because unfortunately, this buy-and-be-happy equation is not as simple it seems. The positive feelings we get when we buy something is only a temporary burst. (Then again, as sad as it sounds, everything in life and life itself is temporary. Only a few things last for hundreds or thousands of years, and even that isn't long when you think about all of human history.)

In the past, I chased tangible items: a nice house, exotic cars, boats, four-wheeled ATVs. I wanted a flat-screen TV on every wall. I thought that if I got these things, then I would be happy. Well, I did get many of them. Did it work? Yes, it did, but only temporarily—only for a few weeks or months. Based on how I felt after such purchases, eventually, I recognized that those tangible items provided only short bursts of satisfaction that wore off pretty quickly. Looking back, I can see that I fought so hard for them and put them on such a high pedestal that they were my ruler and I was their slave.

Other people may have experienced something similar. Consider this example: a young woman is in the market to buy a new car. She goes to the dealership all excited; she can't wait to get the new car she's had her eye on. She ends up going through a long, drawn-out negotiation process, which isn't always the best experience as it can result in added costs. But she overlooks that and remains in a state of excitement, even though getting the car involves making high monthly payments. She tells herself that she can make the payments—if necessary, she will get a second job. For the moment, she convinces herself that these things aren't a problem, because she's so focused on attaining something that she sees as having such a high value, something that's going to make her feel so good if she has it. She seals the deal and gets the car.

But here's what happens next. For the first couple of months, she is really happy and proud...and then that high wears off. It's no longer making her feel the way she thought it would. She's stuck with a big monthly payment that will last a lot longer than the satisfaction she thought the car was going to provide. So, what happens after that point? She seeks yet another high. Financial intelligence was most likely not tapped into here.

This becomes a continuous cycle in people's lives as they run around trying to make themselves feel good by buying things. They feel that money will give them the ultimate satisfaction in life. Our society loves to see all of the millionaires and billionaires smiling as they live a life of luxury. Regular people believe that if they, too, could get those luxury items, then their life would be just as good. But the truth is, money isn't what's making those successful individuals feel good. It may play a part in what they're truly after, but I promise you that money is not their ultimate aim. Having tons of money isn't what makes people like Jeff Bezos (Amazon) and Elon Musk (SpaceX) happy. That's not what gives them satisfaction and fulfillment in life. If they felt that money was the ultimate achievement, they wouldn't be where they are today, which is being focused on making a difference, rather than just making money.

Yes, money helps enable a luxurious lifestyle, but success is not about keeping up with the Joneses the way most people are trying to do within their circles. It's such silly life programming to think that money is a mighty god and that if you have it, you'll be successful and all of your dreams will come true. Let me tell you a little bit about having that mentality: the greats don't think that way. I repeat: the greats don't think that way. People who do think like that may rise at first, but they will eventually fall because they don't have the depth of character to keep them in that higher place. It's not about making money—it's more about making a difference. That's what level the greats are at, money just follows that approach and becomes the reward.

Becoming of value

You might have heard of Jordan Belfort, also known as the "Wolf of Wall Street." If you sat down and had coffee with him today, I bet he would tell you that he had the wrong mindset earlier in his life and that the person he became when he was successful wasn't a person who could stay at the top. Jordan was able to climb at a very fast rate; unfortunately, he declined at a much faster rate. Now, though, Jordan is a successful author who has done a ton of motivational speaking. He is now taking what he has learned—the good and the bad—and passing it along to others to influence their lives in a positive way. He admits that he was wrong back in his "Wolf of Wall Street" days, because back then, all he cared about was generating money when he should have cared about generating value. Creating value in yourself is what you need to focus on if you're going to generate great wealth that's sustainable. So about creating value, we need to understand a little more about what a valuable person is and how to become one.

Let's consider Jim Carrey and how he has gone about his life. He chased his dream and lived every day for something he wanted, namely to become a great actor. I'm sure there were many times when he might have doubted whether that would happen. He was so passionate about it, though, that it was the only thing that filled his mind. He would drive along Mulholland Drive in Los Angeles, California, look out over the city, and visualize the things he wanted in life and the person he wanted to become. Let's stop for a second and think about this— has Jim seemingly answered the three questions I mentioned earlier? Probably.

It appears he knew who he was, he knew what wanted, and he knew why he wanted it. The result has been a success story with great rewards, from fame to money. But was money the driver for Jim? Absolutely not. He wouldn't have been able to overcome the adversity he faced if money had been the big motivator. He had found a passion, something he loved, went in that direction and it created value in himself. I'm sure at the time he had no clue he was making wise moves but him developing as a person from chasing his passion is what did it. He showcased a unique value to the world. He's not going to be thought of as someone who made a lot of money—he will be remembered not only for his great sense of humor, which he showcased through acting, but also his positive effects on others, which he feels is the most valuable currency there is.

Why am I telling you about Jordan Belfort and Jim Carrey? Well, I want you to observe others and understand which directions lead to their success in becoming a person with value, someone who offers their gifts and talents to the world. So first, it's wise to answer the three questions I mentioned earlier, and *then* after that, follow your passion you discover from answering them. Head in that direction my friends.

Unfortunately, the messages we receive in today's society focus only on the fame and money aspects of success. There's not much focus on how success is truly achieved; more importantly, we don't focus on why and how becoming a person of value will lead us to success. But now we can see where true satisfaction in life is found and specifically how the positive feelings we so very much desire to have *is* connected to our passion and our purpose.

Do you think that selecting a career on the basis of what your salary will be is going to bring you good feelings? Or is selecting a career based on its salary going to be one of those times in your life when you only *thought* that's what you wanted because you were unfortunately driven there for the wrong reasons? People who put money first when making career decisions often find out that they hate their job, which often winds up eating up all of their time. Some people even continue this pattern with one unsatisfying job after another...until they finally start looking at the things they're passionate about and head in that direction regardless of the money.

As Kevin Costner's character said in the film *Field of Dreams,* "If you build it, he will come." Think of life in the sense of building upon your desires and becoming who you want to be. The money will come. I can promise you *that* is the secret of success. Very few people accidentally land on the right path toward wealth. Most people are going to jobs every day that they don't like—jobs they might even hate—and are living for the weekends, hoping that's what will bring them satisfaction. I don't want you to have that kind of life. I don't want you to dread your week when Monday comes around, so really look at the three questions and discover your own answers to them. I know deep down you'd enjoy the positive aspects that result in your life after you discover those answers.

Navigation Knowledge

Going after something you love will bring you great wealth and will make you a person of value. Do not chase the money. Always remember that the money will come—it will chase *you* if you chase your passion in life. That's the secret to great wealth.

Our Love & Relationships Pillar

We've covered health and we've covered wealth, so let's move on to the love and relationships pillar. This aspect of life is probably among the first thing I discovered at a young age. Most children have parents or some sort of parental figure to provide for them. During their early years, children are subconsciously connecting with people, and feelings are being generated by these connections. We hope that the feelings and connections would be more often good than bad, but whether or not they are depends on the quality of the people within the child's environment. Unfortunately, that's out of our control since none of us get to pick our parents or caretakers. But when our childhood environments are positive, the feelings we get from our parents or guardians are good feelings, one of the first big "feel-goods" we experience and pick up early on in life.

For a brief moment, I want to step aside from the connections we make as children to point out what also is taking place during this early time of our lives. As children, we become byproducts of our caretakers early on since they are the ones guiding our behavior and teaching us how to get along in life. However, that information can be a blessing or not depending on what that information is and the caregivers' understanding of the correct way to pass it on to their children.

A friend of mine once made a great remark to me that I'll never forget. He said, "Chris, we are becoming a copy of a copy of a copy of a copy." I thought to myself, *Yeah, that does seem to be good.* Thereafter, I started to analyze how I think the later copies are going to turn out. I guess it just all depends on what was presented to the prior copy—what was the data like that was passed on. So many people are bringing new lives into this world so early on, when most of them haven't even figured things out for themselves yet. I'm not trying to bash them in any way; this is simply what I've observed. I can't help but wonder what will be further passed on. As a society, we need to get to the root of the problem, which is making sure that children learn how to navigate life early on in school. Even more importantly, children need to learn how to eat properly so they don't damage their bodies from the start. We need people with healthy bodies and minds, bodies and minds that allow each of us to have a better understanding of life. We need to know that there's more to life than just making and saving money which helps ones navigate better towards the good life.

But when we're young that might be all we get or, our caretakers might pass along well-intentioned comments like "Just be happy!" that don't provide any true meaning or any insight into how to better our lives. Many of us have heard this line at least once in our lives, and I'm pretty sure that hearing it didn't really create any change, because saying "Just be happy!" doesn't explain *how* to be happy or even what "happy" is.

Well to me, happiness is a positive feeling that we want to experience all of the time, but those around us most likely won't provide the answers we seek on how to make happiness happen for us. If the game that Earl Nightingale called "Follow the Follower" is happening here and is going to be played, why not follow an effective follower, one with great life knowledge and results in life? That would be helpful. (Especially to those later copies) But that would require cluing us in when we're still young children and giving us a wise person to follow (or providing children with a better education on life).

Now that's just a bit about us becoming a byproduct, so going back to the connection that we first when we're younger, let's consider that and what happens a little later in life. Let's focus on the most sought-after human relationship, namely being *in love*. What I'm talking about is having a deep connection with another human being— something much more powerful than just being attracted to another person which though is usually involved. We first get a hint of what love is like when we connect as a child with our parents/caretakers, but being "in love" with let's say another that's a non-relative is much different. There's usually a deep connection plus the strong attraction involved together.

Having the kind of connection with another person that usually involves physical attraction is often one of the best "feel-good" experiences we can have. That kind of connection provides a sense of satisfaction that is fundamentally different from the feelings of happiness associated with the purchase of tangible items, such as the short-term high that comes from buying a new car. People may describe this connection in a number of different ways; many say that they met someone who gave off a signal that just drew them to the person. The fact that one person can give us this amazing vibe while another does not comes down to the way each of us was created. Those "good vibes" produce positive feelings that just make us feel good inside. Early on in life, most of us become aware of how good this experience feels; we want this feeling in our lives, and we specifically seek it out. It's usually in grade school that we start to recognize that such a feeling even exists.

The majority of us want to find someone special. Having a partner becomes the main focus of our journey because we want the feelings that associate with that kind of relationship. Nothing else in life has given us such a powerful feeling, so the desire to find that connection becomes the main thing that drives us in life. When this happens, we are blind to the other important aspects of life, such as health and even wealth. Those areas seem to take a back seat to the search for a partner, because the positive feelings the other pillars can provide don't come as quickly, easily, or powerfully as the feelings that come from a relationship with another person do. Plus health and wealth never are a factor young in age so human connection gets greeted first.

Consequently, many people neglect the other areas of life even though they really shouldn't. Being in good health and/or great wealth causes one to feel good—that's a fact. But it's also a fact that none of these feelings may come as quickly, easily, and as strongly as they do when we have a strong connection with another person.

So, let's stop and ask ourselves some questions. Which of these pillars so far do we feel we have the most control over? Which ones are going to be under our complete command, thus allowing us to achieve the great feelings we are trying to give ourselves? Well, let me tell you which one is *not* in our control. You might not like the answer, but it's the "love" one. Think about it. Trying to find someone to be in love with means we are relying on another human being to make us feel good and to forever allow us to continue to have that special feeling. If things shift and the other person changes—

which can easily happen because we cannot control what someone else feels, nor can the person themselves control it—then we lose the positive feelings the relationship provides. We need a counterpart in order to enjoy this feeling, but we *don't* need a counterpart when it comes to the other pillars.

When the good feelings are lost in the relationship scenario, they will be replaced with negative feelings, and we won't like that at all. When we have something great and it's taken away, we experience negative feelings from the loss of that connection. I have mentioned before that things in life are temporary, which is sad when we look at the good things we could lose. But here's the silver lining: negative feelings are also temporary, and they will subside. Please keep that in mind when dealing with dark times.

Everything in life is temporary; everything will eventually be gone or modified from its original form. But I don't want you to think that the connection between you and your partner will inevitably vanish and that you just need to accept that fact. No, that connection could very well continue throughout both of your lives. Yes, as we age, we change, which is why we have no control over things staying the same, but a person *does* have the ability to control *their* actions and thoughts. When both parties make wise decisions, they help their relationship and connection continue to flourish. But of course, we have to hope that our partner will also make wise decisions for our relationship that will protect the connection we have. Since we're on this topic I'll slide in that communication is essential for all relationships, make sure it takes place in yours! So once again, going back to it. This pillar is something that's not in our control, which is why this pillar occupies the third position and not the first or even second.

There are many things in life that we just don't have much control over. If you asked yourself why you like your favorite color, your answer most likely involves feelings (e.g., "Red makes me feel powerful," or "I think blue is calming"), but you didn't really *choose* that color and how it makes you feel. Why do you like certain foods but dislike others? The same thing applies—you may think you've made a conscious decision, but really, the deeper answer is that it wasn't your choice. Your preference comes from how you were originally created and programmed from the start.

Can this change with time? Absolutely. You're always growing and developing, so eventually, you may enjoy a new color or a new food. Why am I telling you this? Because I want you to understand that as much as you love the connection that another person can give you, you have no control over the future, because like you, that person will also continue to develop throughout life. Development brings change for both of you. For example, I used to love playing video games, but at this point in my life, I don't have the same passion for this activity. Nowadays, since things change—and often in unexpected ways—I enjoy writing. That's growth which is change.

Still, the majority of people seem to focus on finding love as their #1 goal in life. But what do they think is going to happen to them if that connection fades and goes away? What will they have to fall back on? Nothing, most likely. And that's why it's wise to learn, first and foremost, how to make yourself feel good without relying on another person. Today, the divorce rate is through the roof—well over 50% of marriages end in divorce. When that happens and people lose the good feelings they got from that relationship, they experience terrible heartache and have trouble coping. The one positive result I've noticed is that many people do eventually go back to their true priority, which is often getting back in shape, because they neglected their health and they want to feel good about themselves again. Some go back to school to achieve the degree they wanted, a degree that could result in them gaining more wealth. Health and wealth seemed to have been put on hold as far as great attention during their marriages because a loving relationship was the main driver that made them feel good.

The bottom line is that we must make ourselves feel good first, well before we rely on a love life to make us happy. Health and wealth give us a solid foundation to build upon. If we have them and our relationship does fade away, we have a strong structure to fall back upon. We won't fall as hard, and our recovery won't be as difficult. We won't be walking through life with negativity that in turn becomes a poisonous cycle that affects others as well as ourselves. If our bodies are running at top-notch efficiency, we can handle stress more easily. (Great health) If our bodies are being polluted—which causes stress on the body—and then a difficult life event hits us, what do you think the result will be? It will be bad, my friend. Unfortunately, many people may have already experienced this, and that I'm truly sorry for.

I want to emphasize that I'm *not* advising you to hold off on love, not by any means. Definitely engage with someone who interests you. Just don't neglect the first two pillars. Remember, the first pillar is your health. The second involves answering the three questions about yourself so that you'll have a direction to go towards that can generate wealth, a direction backed up by your passion. All of us need to have faith in that pillar, because it will lead to great wealth and success and great feelings. We have the most control over these two pillars. If we rely solely on the good feelings that another person provides, we won't have anything to fall back on. The fall will be a rough one and will probably be accompanied by regret. A fence that goes up easily will fall down easily. Likewise, finding someone who makes you feel good is fairly easy, but that situation can also easily fall/fade.

It's unlikely that the third pillar will keep us alive and well all by itself. We shouldn't rely on just external factors to make ourselves feel good. It's best to tackle the first two pillars, then add number three to the mix. At that point, we feel more control of achieving positive outcomes—we feel like we're living as we were meant to live. We're in a better position and ready to truly enjoy affection from another person. And the other person will enjoy us—an amazing person who has our entire body running at optimal levels, showcasing the beauty we were meant to showcase and moving forward in life with a direction powered by our passion, a direction that leads us to our purpose. One of much success.

Someone who has that kind of structure in their life is lighting themselves up inside. Who wouldn't want to be around them? They're magnetic to anyone in their atmosphere, especially their partner, who's enjoying the company of a well-balanced individual. You know the partner will feel good, too, and kick those good feelings back to you! There goes that balance taking place again. But yes, that's how true connections are made. Never settle for less than being with a person who positively affects you so strongly, someone whose positivity you reciprocate. You *deserve* that person!

You'll enjoy the results of the third pillar much more when you've given the first two pillars proper attention. This is just one of ways I've chosen to play the game of life.

Navigation Knowledge

Being in love is great, but understand that it requires another person for you to generate those good feelings, and unfortunately, we have less control over someone else's feelings towards us. Hopefully, both people will have wise thoughts and make good decisions to keep the connection strong. Just remember that you should never neglect your health and wealth pillars—don't rely solely on just the third "love & relationships" pillar to feel good.

Our Fulfillment Pillar

The progress we make with the first three pillars can really influence our results in the last pillar, which is fulfillment. Tai Lopez, the business adviser I mentioned earlier, shared with me that if you want the good life, you must focus on the four main pillars: health, wealth, love, and happiness or what some call fulfillment. I've thought about those pillars quite a bit, and I've realized that we're more likely to achieve good feelings in life when we have balance and pursue all four pillars. This fourth pillar can be influenced by the first three, but also includes what one might call bonus rounds, i.e., other aspects of life that can help one find fulfillment.

One of the strongest aspects of the fulfillment pillar I feel is friendships, which tie into the third pillar because friendships also provide a sense of connection. Having love for someone is a great thing and creates strong feelings. (Of course, as we all know, being *in love* seems to be at another level.) The good feelings you get from being around your friends can make a huge contribution to your sense of fulfillment in life. And also, on the other hand, losing a connection—whether it's a connection to a friend or a lover—can be a big loss and can affect you more severely if you have neglected the first and second pillars as I have mentioned.

Along with friendships, there are other little-but-big things that make us feel good. These smaller things may not give us a long-lasting high, but they certainly assist in creating life balance. One can almost always turn to these things when life maybe isn't feeling as zestful as we'd like.

Some of these things are traveling and going places, watching a television show we love, going to the movies, having a night out on the town, reading a book, enjoying the holidays, spending time with our pets, and enjoying any other activities we like to pursue. These are just a few of the "extras" in life. (A close friend of mine always directs me to focus on these little things in life and use them to fill in the gaps while I'm climbing my mountain.) That short list only touches on a few of the "extras"—you could also include the sight of trees arching over your head and the sound of birds chirping. But at the risk of sounding repetitive as I've been, if we neglect our health, these activities won't be as appealing anymore. My apologies for constantly mentioning health, but it's just so very crucial, because it's what allows the "feel-greats" to happen. Being in optimal health really should be our main goal.

We can find fulfillment and happiness in lots of ways, but just that fourth pillar alone won't give us the happiness we seek. Our happiness depends on the other pillars, too. When we embrace all of them, we have the ability to feel positive emotions on a continuous basis. That, my friends, is living. Living the way I'm sure everyone truly desires, living in a way that allows us to pursue the happiness people always say they want, the good feelings we're forever chasing.

Cheers to the higher power at play and our creator! The body's ability to feel good may just be the most precious and valuable thing we have. Feeling good is our main goal in life, so let's continue to think about more ways we can make that happen naturally.

Navigation Knowledge

The fulfillment pillar is made up of your main three pillars and also those little things in life. Make sure you dedicate some time to enjoying those little things. Those instant highs have a place in the overall picture—they will help create balance and fill in some of the rough spots on your journey.

Basic Summary of a Person's Life

- You were created and dropped off here on earth with zero knowledge.

- You obtain knowledge from others and from things in your environment by sight, sound, touch, smell, and taste.

- Your ultimate root goal in life is to feel good while you are here.

- Good feelings are produced by your body ("good feelings" are connected to "being in good health").

- You are uniquely created and have been programmed with a custom set of interests in life that will give you a "feel-good" response if and when you obtain them. The drive to achieve them is what's lingering behind all of your daily decisions.

Okay, so you've learned about the four main pillars and now have a better understanding of our unique life. In order to achieve the good life we all want, we have to give the pillars our attention (and more of it!). Now it's time to go a bit deeper. The knowledge I'm about to share now has helped me and will help you navigate through life as you work on your pillars. The information will enhance ones mindset to better assist with operating life.

Independent Thinking

Our beliefs, well they mostly stem from other people, although we do learn some things from our own experiences: like if we fall down, it hurts; if we're stung by a bee, we can wind up with a welt or even an allergic reaction. We can think of those as environmental lessons. But the bulk of the programming we pick up (especially early on) comes from information that's delivered by the people around us. Most of those people are much older and have been around a lot longer than we have, like parents or teachers. Our friends also play a role since they share what they know, too. That's how we become a byproduct of our environment.

But what I think is particularly interesting is that not many people question what they are learning or come up with their own thoughts about life. We tend to trust that the people delivering insights to us have figured things out...but have they? Where did they get all their information? Did they get it the same way, i.e., mostly delivered by those before them? Many can agree that even the media probably plays a huge roll in educating the minds. But did anyone along the way ever question what they were told and at times tap into great thoughts of their own? The great American radio speaker and philosopher from the 1950s, Earl Nightingale, was probably right when decades ago, he said that he felt there's a game being played in America, and that game is called "Follow the Follower." (You may recall that I previously mentioned this.) When I heard him say that, I paused his audio session and really started to analyze what he had just said. Within minutes, I felt like he was exactly right: pretty much everyone is following what everyone else is doing. The majority of people simply conform to societal standards rather than being independent thinkers going in their own direction.

As I sat there, I remembered a friend of mine who had recently come to me, saying that he had a great idea. It seems like we all eventually have that "great idea" at some point, right? But just having an idea only does so much, because the work involved in making that idea into reality—the adversity that needs to be overcome—is really the hard part. However, my friend was very excited about his idea, and I was willing to help him get started on it.

During the first week, I helped him create a roadmap and go over the basics of bringing his idea to life. We made great progress; and at the time, I really felt that he was very passionate about his idea. But then the weekend came around, and something changed. The very next week, he stopped by my office to visit me. As always, we first chatted about the weekend, but then I changed the topic to the project we were working on...and instantly, I could see by his body language that his feelings had changed. The first thing he said was, "Yeah...I don't know, man."

I asked him what he meant by that as he'd originally been really excited about his idea. He said, "Well, I was out the other night and was talking to some people and I don't know if it's a good idea anymore."

I asked him why would it matter what other people believe? Why would you need their approval? I mean, they might not see what you see; they might not be visionaries.

He said, "Well, they told me that they have already seen stuff out there like it, so I kind of got bummed out."

That's when I got quiet. *Wow!* I was thinking. *Just a few days ago, this guy was a believer, but then a couple of people who didn't like his idea killed it for him. I wonder if he even thought about who was giving him feedback? Have they ever created anything from a passionate idea?* I couldn't understand why on earth my friend would not recognize that it doesn't matter what other people think, because they most likely don't see his vision or his dream. I asked my friend, "Where were you when you ran into them?"

He replied, "Oh, I was at the local bar—the one around the corner."

I said, "Who cares if their feedback was negative, especially if you believe in your idea? Why would you need their approval?"

He said, "Yeah, I guess you're right." Then the topic changed and we started chatting about other things.
But here's the thing, he had stopped believing in his idea. It got killed by some random people at a bar. Even after I shared my thoughts, nothing really changed—what he heard was enough to kill his drive for his idea. It's been years since that conversation, and I can now say that I don't think he should have invested any further in it. Not because he didn't have a good idea—I just think he wasn't passionate enough about it. Maybe he just wanted to make money, which is a terrible internal driver. Maybe he had other reasons. Who knows? What I do know is that it takes love and passion to really bring an idea to life. *Those* are the drivers. I know that from younger myself as I chased money early on with no real passion. It also takes being an independent thinker who is not persuaded by the views of others, especially when adversity

hits...which it will. It will probably hit 50 to 100 times before one's idea becomes a reality. From personal experience, I know that it takes much more than just the desire to make some money to make an idea into a reality. My friend's mindset was shifted quickly, not by difficulty, but just by a hint of doubt that entered his mind from the feedback he received. Being an independent thinker driven by love and passion and not by money keeps us moving forward and prevents us from easily experiencing doubt.

Unfortunately, the majority of people have been conditioned *not* to believe in themselves, but rather to listen to others and follow. This goes back to what was being passed on to them early on, along with an unfortunate tendency to dwell on failures in life. They weren't taught otherwise; they weren't taught how to look at so-called "failures" in a healthy way. Not one that leads to asking others for their thoughts and approval rather one believing in themselves. Being independent thinkers who trust ourselves and our own thoughts seems to be a rare thing today. I strongly recommend having faith in yourself instead of constantly asking others for directions, leading one to get more and more caught up just like other followers.

During Earl Nightingale's audio session, he also mentioned a survey conducted back in the 1950s that had asked 20 people why they got up for work in the morning. Nineteen out of the twenty stated, "Well, everyone works," and couldn't even explain why they did (aside from needing to make money). It's kind of baffling, but that goes to show the way most people simply conform—many are just following one another with zero direction from their own thoughts.

My question to you is this: are you following and listening to people who are going where you want to go? Do they showcase the results that you want to get, too, or are they missing that part yet still talk as if they know what's best? The bulk of information we listen to should come from our own research or experiences. It's good to be cautious of what we hear from others and even the media (more on that soon).

For example, most information is delivered in a standardized, generic, "right" way. But what I'm talking about in this book regarding life, offers genuine information that can really help lead a person to success. I have put much thought into my own struggles and what I have gone through and also into my successes. I feel like a guinea pig who is now is sharing what I've learned with others. For me, every day has been about trying to build a good life. As I've said to my brother, it's okay to hear people, but if you choose to listen to them and take their advice, I'd first look at the results they are getting from life.

That said, there are some exceptions—very few, but they exist—when people do know the way even though they haven't yet showcased great results. One example of that is sports, where often, average athletes become phenomenal coaches. (One could attribute a large part of that to physical genetics, plus being mentally well-equipped to achieve their eventual success.) But it's rare.

We have all listened to the advice of others and have followed their guidance. I'm sure most of us have heard something along these lines:
"You need to go to college. You need to do well there and get a degree, because if you don't, you will struggle in life.

Also, be sure to save money. Remember: save, save, save, save."

But let's stop and think about that for a second. Is that really the best path for everyone in life? That path's result is pretty much all around us if one is curious where they'd end up. It's the direction most people take and really the one that we all have stuck in our head to follow. Just as we're told to focus on getting good grades. My mother used to get so upset with me when I brought home poor grades. She would constantly say, "You need to go to school and get good grades, Chris." Which I understand completely why now.

She was programmed to think that I would be a failure in life if I didn't get those good grades, and that bothered her. I recall the day when I started to question this whole "getting good grades" thing. What if I went to school and didn't do that? Obviously, I wouldn't graduate from high school or be able to obtain a college degree. I had been internally programmed to believe that doing poorly in school meant I wouldn't be successful in life. But if we looked at Forbes Billionaire list we'd find leaders of the world paved their own way without schooling being the huge factor behind their success. Now many people talk about how smart their child is and how good their grades are which they're proud of and I get it as they should, but all in all, do the grades we get even matter?

Once I thought so, but years later, my answer to that is no, it doesn't matter. Not defining success in life which is what we are trying to get the most out of here. I'm sure many will disagree with me which is fine. It's just because everyone is still being conditioned to think that good grades mean something in this world. Most parents, not all feel that good grades almost guarantee that their kid will be a success. But once again, let's stop and think about that. Is that really true? No, not at all. All of the tests and quizzes we take are just a bunch of random information that we will eventually forget and not use later in life. The bulk isn't information close to anything to do with living life. It's just basic information all around.

Our school system appears to be broken in a way. We have mostly, not all, average people guiding humans to also be equally average. We ram outdated information into students. Those textbooks are not going to truly help us out in life, I can tell you that. Once most of us have completed high school and graduate, we still have no clue as to what we really want to do. Personally, I was up in the air in terms of what I wanted. My mother encouraged me to go to college, so I tried doing that for a while. It wasn't for me, though—I had no interest in what was going on in the classroom. Deep down, I felt that college wasn't right for me, and I pulled away from that direction.

Now, don't get me wrong—I'm not against education. I *am* against the kind of schooling that's being delivered right now because I think it doesn't really help people in their overall lives. Instead, I support helping each young person find their path in life. I support a higher level of learning outside of those silly textbooks. I support having classes that focus on how to navigate life the best possible way for each unique person. There's so much education outside of math, history, English, science, and economics. It would have been nice to hold off on reading literature like King Lear and instead maybe go over ways to invest money. I think that would be a bit more helpful to others in my opinion. What's happening is teachers are guiding us to follow the suit of the average safe path like many to mediocrity. I don't think it's their fault, they're just following the system.

Now that I am older, I'm definitely looking at life much differently. I feel teachers should be paid much more but also require higher qualifications to land their jobs. The best of the best should selected as they're the ones educating humanity, helping pave the way toward our future.

If we look at what's happening right now throughout the United States, people are being programmed to think that the system is the way. Also encouraged to take the safe road in life, a road that is built on the fear of losing rather than on the desire to win and thrive. We're playing defense more so and living in fear versus playing offense and having faith in ourselves.

I'd like to pause for a moment here to say that I think America is an amazing country. I love it dearly. I'm so thankful to be here and to have the freedom to go after my dreams. Living in America allows me to create the life that I truly want and strive to be the person I want to be without much limitations. It's just that I feel that the way I was guided and driven early on in life was very poor—I was set up to live a life devoid of much meaning, a life that was filled with the basic day-to-day concerns of living. In other words, I was brought up like everyone else. But I didn't want that kind of humdrum life—it depressed me. Inside, I've always had a fire burning to become more alive.

Recently, I have traveled and visited many countries to see

what their basic day-to-day living is all about. I've seen that it's mostly operating in that fourth pillar and enjoying the small day-to-day things. By no means do I feel that's ultimately a bad thing, no, but I do feel that there are more pillars that people should pay attention to if they want the good life and not just a decent life.

Of course, we all are built differently and should tailor our individual paths to suit our unique selves. For someone like me who wants more and is willing to work for it, I need to go down another path, one that may offer great resistance but also great rewards. There're other people out there as well that may wish to pursue that path, too. Those guiding the way have no clue what is going on inside of me or others who shouldn't be limited and educated toward the basic. That just sets us up to become average unless we somehow wake ourselves up and break away from the pack. Which this book may help in doing that for you.

All of us should be presented with a complete map of potential life directions based on different mindsets. We shouldn't all adjust to just one way of living. That way may support some of us, but not others. Steering clear of talking about dreaming what's possible and instead focusing strictly on following the path of the system is an easy way to limit our dreams. Go to school... Graduate... Go to college... Get a degree... Get a job... Get married... Buy a house... Start a family... Go to barbeques and birthday parties... And then unfortunately, pass away. I'm sorry but some of us need more meaning than that.

Many of the people I went to school with are on the path I just mentioned. In school, I recall them doing very well, much better than I did. They would bring home exceptional grades while I was viewed as more of a failure since I didn't get good grades. Soon after high school, they went off to college and I did not—I went off to a job. However, that was one of the most powerful educational experiences of my life. I was blessed to see what young entrepreneurs were getting out of life and then was able to compare that to the kind of life my parents and teachers were guiding me towards. Years later, those students who performed much better than I did in school aren't in positions that I think they themselves thought they would be in.

That's what made me start to question that path that many have taken. If they had been independent thinkers and had done what they felt was right for themselves and not just what they were told to do, maybe they would be in a better position now. That's very much possible to do if we stop and question things and spend time thinking about the direction we're told we should go. The truth is, the kind of education most of us get results in the majority of people living paycheck to paycheck, which surely isn't comfortable.

Fortunately, because I was able to observe young entrepreneurs whom I was able to be around in my later teenage years, I learned that they weren't just doing what others told them to do—they were thinking for themselves and paving their own way. My boss at the time was 24 years old and became a multi-millionaire right in front of me, all because he understood how to play the field to bring him great wealth. He was an independent thinker. When I was 19, he slowly but surely taught me to be an independent thinker, too, instead of just conforming to the status quo. That's when my life shifted.

Navigation Knowledge

Become an independent thinker and start to question what is being delivered to you. The education we receive early on doesn't appear to set us up for the good life. The choice is yours if you want to break away from 95% of the population and mold life to your liking, but doing so starts within the mind; it starts when you begin looking at life from another angle. *Your* angle, not someone else's.

Deciding What it Is

Without even knowing you, I know there are things you would like to have happen in your life. Discovering your interests is what's going to give you a direction in life that will be extremely satisfying and give you those "feel-good" feelings. It's very common for those interests to be linked to your goals, which ultimately becomes a reason to get up in the morning. If we don't discover our interests and if we don't set goals, we can definitely become lost in life.

As an example, let's take a boat for instance. Imagine a boat heading out to sea on the way to a wonderful destination. This boat is likely to get there because there's a captain of the boat who has a map and GPS system and who is focused on the goal, i.e., arriving at the destination. But imagine if we now take away the captain, map, and GPS from the boat. There's no telling where that boat will end up now. It will probably end up the way many of us do: being pushed around by life, like random waves and currents towards that boat. We'll get sent in a direction we didn't plan on or desire, and we can wind up getting lost in life or like a boat eventually becoming shipwrecked.

I bring this up because everyone should stop and look at their life for a moment. Unfortunately, many of us have no plans and no goals, and that leads to having no direction, which can easily result in life handing us what *it* wants rather than what *we* want. But let's say that just like the boat, we have the proper things in place. We have our captain, our map, and our GPS, and we know exactly where we want to end up. It's safe to say there's a high probability our boat (our life) will end up at or at least near our intended destination.

This same logic can apply to a person who knows what they want and has a list of their interests and goals. As long as they take action and move forward, there's a strong chance they will arrive at their destination as well. We must understand like a boat met with unexpected weather, a person will encounter obstacles as well as they make their way to their destination. This is expected, but having a belief that they'll get there and being well aware of the overall journey and stages will help them persevere (more on that later).

So, here we are at the starting line. We need to decide what we want to happen. Feel free to stop reading for a second and think about what it is you want. If one recalls, this is that second question from the wealth pillar section. Go into a quiet room and just think about what you want to have happen in your life within the time you have been given. And shortly after, just like it was shown in the law of attraction book/movie "The Secret." I suggest one to put what they want down on paper. One must either write it down or type it and print it out, and then showcase what they want their life to become. It allows one to look at everything like it's a big map. Then place these goals somewhere where you will see them daily—it does no good to just have them sitting in your memory, where you may only think of your goals from time to time. I say this as I once came across this interesting *Forbes* 1979 Harvard MBA program study that can be found online and it showed astonishing results when putting down on paper and not left in one's mind.

You see, our life can just pass us by and distractions can easily consume us to the point that we wake up one day wondering what the heck happened in life. And that happens because we're constantly distracted and never focus on what we really want. The result? We end up not getting what we want. We need to be aware of our goals and focused on what we want. We need to give attention to what we want. It's a huge part of winning at this game of life.

In the next section, I'm going to share some examples to help you zone in on what you want to have happen in your life. Please remember that it doesn't matter how far-fetched your goals might be—just put them on the list. Don't be embarrassed if they sound crazy. This is your list for you; whether you share it with anyone else is completely your choice. This is between you and your higher power. Just have faith and believe that things *are* possible. Remember, about 95% of people are not doing that. Let's separate you from the pack and trust that your creator will show you what is possible for you.

Also, please never forget that the term "impossible" was created by a human. Nothing is impossible. There is always a way. Just because a human doesn't see the way doesn't mean one doesn't exist. Wherever you are right now, I want you to do something for me. Imagine zooming out from the earth and into the sky. In your mind, you should be just about drifting off into space. What you see is the earth right in front of you, slowly spinning. We must never forget, that right there, is possible. Something much bigger taking place and happening than our ideas, that down here on earth, seem impossible. There are no limits on earth or out in the universe, just possibilities. Anyone can have what they want—they just have to apply themselves and understand the playing field and how to work it.

As the new independent thinker you should now be becoming, please don't ever let others shower you with doubt and disbelief. Please don't ever let others dissuade you from pursuing your dreams. The truth is that the human brain is only so smart, and the smartest thing any of us could accept is the fact that we don't know everything. How things work and govern this earth, well we can only try to connect the dots as best as we can. Why are we here? What's our purpose? Well, only the originator knows that. Even Socrates once said, "I know nothing except the fact of my ignorance."

There have been many great minds, but at the end of the day, we dictate what is possible or not in our own minds. Remember that he who says he can and he who says he can't are both usually right. So go for what you want. Trust that your interests and the things in your heart were given to you for a reason. You didn't get to choose these things. Have faith and work toward bringing them to life, and I promise you'll receive help along the way. Science says "Show me, and I'll believe." Faith says "Believe, and I'll show you."

A great example of faith leading to success goes way back to 1903, when two brothers by the names of Orville and Wilbur Wright were finally able to build the first successful airplane. In the years prior to that, they had created and tested gliders to analyze how this new flying machine could become a reality. During this phase of the development, not many people were interested in what they were doing—they didn't see any value in it. That didn't bother the Wright Brothers, though.

Their first successful flight was with the Kitty Hawk on December 17th of 1903. Looking back, you'd think that was a memorable date, but at the time, only five people showed up to view the flight. Many people thought that what the brothers were doing just didn't have any purpose; others were very skeptical in general. When the brothers offered their airplane to the US government, officials initially responded that they had no interest in such a flying machine. But that was then, and this is now. Here we are today with planes flying all over the world and shuttles even being sent to space!

There are those who believe in what's possible and those who support the *im*possible. I personally feel there is always a way to make our dreams happen. When we look at the Wright Brothers, it's clear they felt the same way, too.

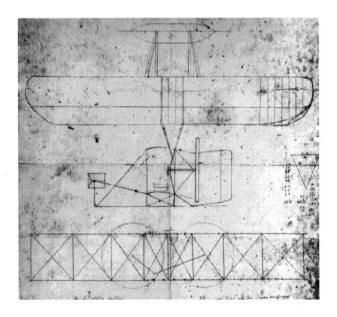

So like you see what the Wright Brothers did, let's put our dreams down on paper. If we want the good life to happen, we need to take this step. Please keep in mind that we have to write down what we *want* and not what we *don't* want.

Always focus on the positive in life—never give attention to the negative. That's something we should all remember.

What Matters the Most

If you're still kind of up in the air on what exactly you want to happen in life, that's fine. Let's review the main areas again that matter the most—that should give you an idea of what to think about. The goal is to achieve at least one thing from each category, but by all means, don't let that idea limit you. There's truly no limit. So here they are again...

- Health
- Wealth
- Love & Relationships
- General Fulfillment

Some people might fill up one category more than others, and that's fine. The goal is not just to fill them up, but to give each pillar attention by taking action. I feel like a good level to strive for is to get a 7 or higher in each pillar. Remember, even if we filled up one pillar to the complete maximum, we could still be living an unfulfilling life due to an imbalance with the other areas. Just because we have gained financial independence, we could still have poor health and poor relationships, for example. We could be so absorbed by chasing money and making money that we ignore all of the other areas. (I have been guilty of this myself.) But if no attention is given to those other areas and we're essentially unbalanced, we can't be surprised when no one wants to be near us because they don't like the person we have become. Possibly because we're money driven only. We might no longer have friends to hang out with; we might no longer have someone to talk to. It's wise that we really do give all of these areas in life our full attention.

Remember me talking about money being put on a pedestal? Saying that it can cloud our mind and distract one from focusing on the other areas of life that need their attention? Please do your best to not let that happen to you—go within and figure out your passion in life. Please think about each pillar and grab a bit of interest from each.

Below are some examples you can use to establish some helpful thoughts.

Health

One of the things I have written down is that I want to have the healthiest body, mind, and spirit one can possess. This is directly connected to my overall health. Health is my #1 goal. I know that if I want to go the distance and live an extraordinary life, I need to be operating at a top-notch level. I highly recommend that others strive for the same.

Wealth

A good friend of mine has written down that she wants multiple streams of income, including residuals coming in from different sources. If that's something you desire, too, write it down. If you can be even more specific, that's even better—for example, you might specify multiple streams from an online business. The more specific, the better.

Love & Relationships

If you want to have more relationships or stronger relationships, write that down. If you want to find love, romance, or any kind of relationship, write that down. Maybe you want to be married and start a family. Heck, even write down how you envision your partner would look and act! A friend of mine had done that, and so had her eventual partner. They found each other, and they're together now. I was blown away.

Fulfillment

Let's say you want to travel more, or play sports, or enjoy your hobbies. Maybe you want to spend more time painting or hanging out with friends. Write that down. As I'm writing and editing this book, it's October 6th of 2018. I've been paying a lot of attention to the fulfillment pillar lately. It was my weakest pillar, but that all changed. I've been travelling a lot, too—my friends keep calling me "Mr. Worldwide" and "Mr. International." It feels good knowing that I'm living life on my terms. That, plus the feedback I'm receiving from others lets me know that I'm playing it right. Just how I want you to play it.

As you write down your goals in all of these areas of life, imagine you're painting a picture of your life. Better yet, think of the process as creating your biopic or biography. Everyone's life should be a story, and an awesome one at that. You're giving yourself a direction, a path in life, a path with meaning. If you want to be a movie director, go for it! If you want to be a musician, write that down. Whatever it is you want, write it down. Believe in it. Have faith in it. Give it attention by taking action. It *will* come to life. Heck, the Wright Brothers did.

Navigation Knowledge

Writing down what you want to happen in all of the pillars of your life creates a map that will get you there. You are your own captain, and it's up to you to give attention to the map and have faith that it will guide you to the destination you seek.

Becoming a Visionary Daily

What I mean by "becoming a visionary" is really just to visualize what it is you want to happen in your life. All the desires that one puts down on paper should then receive the power of thought. The more we keep visualizing ourselves becoming the person we want to become or having the life we want to have, the more likely we'll be able to attain that vision. There's no limit to visualizing—one may do it as often as they like.

I'll use myself as an example. No matter what day it is or whether it's a holiday or workday, I'm usually visualizing my future. I constantly think about the person I'm going to become, the car I will be driving, the home I will have, and even the woman I plan to marry.

These constant thoughts I play out in my head also do something else: they make me feel good. Why wouldn't they right? I'm creating positive thoughts about something I desire. That's just another added bonus to one that's visualizing. One might think I'm obsessed with visualizing, and that may be true. But then I think to myself, *Maybe I'm just not distracted by the world around me; maybe I'm just very focused on my own life.* I've answered the three big questions about what I want to happen during the time I am here on earth. Since I know what my answers are, which are things that make me happy and what I want from life. Well my mind now naturally drifts to those desires happening in the future without me even trying. Also, I'm drifting away to a positive state of mind, which is certainly great for one's health.

The other day I noticed it's a new habit where I'm not even

forcing myself to visualize anymore—I want these things to come to fruition so badly that I automatically tap into them every day. Most commonly, I visualize when I'm driving or taking a shower. I'm sharing this with you because if and when this starts happening to you, then you'll know you have truly found what you want. So many time's people have told me that they have no clue what they really want from life. Its unfortunate, but I always encourage one to turn within by tapping inside themselves to find those answers. I can only share what I have done and provide these tips to help you. We all must do our best to figure out what it is we want, because *that's* what we will be giving our attention to.

Once one does, soon enough, their mind will start drifting to what they want randomly, which in turn results in a person constantly giving their dreams attention. It's an amazing habit to create. One won't be able to stop thinking about the positive results they'll get from life.

So, what happens when one does this for themselves, why am I encouraging those to create this visionary habit? Well, as Jeff Bezo's the founder of Amazon, I like to work with the laws of physics and not against them. Here's a look at two important laws on earth, and personally two of my favorites. The first law goes hand in hand with visualizing.

Law of Attraction

This law supports that where our attention goes, our energy flows. What we seek in life is seeking us. And why not, as I've pointed out earlier one didn't get to personally select their interest in life, it's how they were created. If one chooses to follow what lies within them, life will meet them halfway. All of ones dreams and desires will be there at the halfway point. The middle is where balance can exist, and that's exactly what the universe seeks. When we give the pillars, goals, things in life attention, by not only thought but massive action. (which we will go over later in Give it Attention) The law of attraction starts to work in a person's favor in terms of manifestation. This is why I'm big on visualizing—trusting the great discoveries of the physicist before my time. It allows me to be in a constant state of the person I want to become and *do* what I am going do in this world before I depart.

When we put down everything on paper (or even create a vision board), we help the law of attraction happen. Placing your goals somewhere where you can see them daily can be very beneficial to generating more positive thoughts. Remember, it's very easy to get distracted. So what I did was make my goals hit me right in the face whenever I walk through my front door. Prior to that, my original vision board was at my work desk, which is where I spent long hours. Our constant thoughts and images feed our subconscious and help us manifest our desires. Earl Nightingale again, once shared something that he felt was the greatest secret to achieving this, and what that simple was, well,

"We become what we think about."

Thoughts becoming things which seems to tie right into the law of attraction. Visualizing where we're going in life daily, whether those visualizations come from random thoughts or during meditation, will help one attain their goals.

Law of Balance

As I mentioned in the foreword, one will come to understand the law of balance plays a big role when attention is given to all four pillars. If we think about pretty much everything in this world that was not created by humans, we notice that there's always an opposite. For example, where there's up, there's down; where there's left, there's right. There's hot and cold, dark and light, smooth and rough, short and tall. When we look at those pairings, we notice that they are actually one and that they're connected: there cannot be one without the other. There's also a halfway point where one becomes the other. You can see that on the bar graph, where I've used hot and cold as an example. The central point creates an equal side on the opposite ends, giving the pairing its balance.

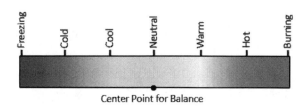

Center Point for Balance

While keeping balance in mind, let's look at a few more examples along with some created by humanity.

If a shelf were not balanced would it function properly? Well depending on the angle, it would not. Certain items may slide off of it if it becomes too unbalanced.

Have you ever seen what happens to a ceiling fan when it's

missing a blade which causes it to be unbalanced? It wobbles all over the place and doesn't function properly. Just like a car with unbalanced tires which would cause them not to rotate properly and interrupt its function.

Here's an interesting one. A person's blood or oxygen levels in their body. There's a certain level that our blood cells need to be at otherwise if they are too high or too low it would cause problems in our system. The result is usually not a good one.

If our equilibrium is off, our balance is off and we have problems walking as a person. And here's something else that always needs to be in balance: liquid. It can be moved around at many angles but seems to always find its balance here on earth.

And speaking of earth, I have come across a reading regarding the earth and its axis seeming to shift at times. A study performed at Princeton University feels that this adjustment is taking place to restore its balance. Whether inner or surface changes of weight disruption, it corrects itself.

As a believer in the law of balance, I find this theory to be one I support.

But why I am talking about the law of balance? What does this have to do with navigating life?

Well, the answer is quite simple, although it may require one to have great faith in something much bigger than ourselves. I've pointed out just a couple of things related to balance. What seems to be is that the universe demands balance. If someone fills up one side of the scale or gives positive effort (i.e., attention) and thoughts to certain areas of life, those areas will fill up for that individual. If one projects not just positivity but maybe negativity, remember that will that also will be returned. It's wise to be careful what one throws out.

Balance plays a role in our world and seems to happen in many ways. Things operate best when they are in harmony. If someone does bad things, it's just a matter of time before the universe disciplines that individual and tries to straighten them up. It's called karma: what goes around, comes around. If one neglects their health pillar, well, their health will neglect them. Balance occurs.

With this in mind, I'm cautious about what I throw out to others—I know it will boomerang back to me. Also, I purposely tilt the scale by giving a massive effort, knowing that if I create an unbalance with my positive effort towards something, it has to balance back—the reward I seek from giving is on its way. However, one must be patient and hold on to faith in order for this magic to happen. We can't expect instant gratification or results, because things sometimes take time, especially things of great value. Those require far more effort and rarely come to fruition quickly. Be aware of that and have faith that a balance must take place and that your hard efforts will be rewarded.

Remember again, science says, "Show me, and I'll believe." Faith says, "Believe, and I'll show you."

🗺 *Navigation Knowledge*

When we create a habit of visualizing and when we focus daily on the positive goals we've set out to achieve, we ignite the power of the laws of physics to work in our favor. What do we have to lose? Nothing. But what do we have to gain? Everything! It's time to have faith in what's possible my friends.

Easy Goals vs. Hard Goals

When we pursue goals in life, we notice that from start to finish, some goals have very few obstacles compared to others. The ones with less obstacles or resistance I label as being "easy." The more "difficult" ones are going to have many more obstacles, and those obstacles become stages that one will go through. As you've probably heard before, "If something were easy, then everybody would do it." And when everybody can do it, then it becomes less of value due to saturation.

What this represents is a form of supply and demand. As an example, let's look at being a cashier job wise. This is no offense to anyone who is a cashier—I just want to use this as an example. Most cashiers today use advanced computer systems to do their jobs. These systems require very minimal labor or skills from their operators, so the job itself becomes an easy one, and many people then qualify for the position. Consequently, the income for that position—the reward—becomes less of value. Also the fact that the supply of potential cashiers for such job is so great that it causes the reward to be low.

Obviously, depending on the area one lives there may be a shortage of job supply or maybe even a medium supply which may raise the value a bit. But either way the amount of people there are available on earth or in the United States out tilt the scale by far. This is what causes the reward to be low for an easy task or even many goals especially with a high supply.

Having this understanding of supply and demand is helpful,

because it's valid for just about anything in life. Whether we're talking about health, wealth, love, or fulfillment, if you do what's easy, expect less of a feel-good reward. That brings to mind a great quote I once heard from the motivational speaker Les Brown: "If you do what's easy in life, your life will be hard. If you do what's hard, your life will be easy."

Let's say you want to be in amazing shape, with a toned body and ripped abs. If you want such a reward, you'll have to really stick to a proper diet and thorough training. If you want an average body type, there's much less work to do; the obstacles and level of difficulty decreases.

Or say you want to write your own book someday. Well, completing a book and being an author isn't an easy task—it takes great thought and hours and hours of writing. The reward, though, is remarkable: now you have a tangible item that can offer entertainment and/or knowledge to others and income generating for you, plus being an author gives you added credibility. But because writing a book is difficult and not many people do it, being an author offers great value due to a low supply.

Another example is relationships. If two people want to have a loving relationship but do what's easy and don't give it much effort, well, their reward will be less. They might still have a relationship, but their connection won't be as strong. If they want the relationship to be more than that, both parties need to put in more effort and do things like resolve disagreements, be willing to work on themselves as individuals, etc.

I'm sorry to say this, but none of us were created to operate in harmony at all times—we all have developed unbalanced habits as a byproduct of our environments. Some of these habits can and will stand in the way of attaining our goals in life, and we need to work on changing those habits in order to be successful. In terms of relationships, many people have trouble expressing how they feel toward their partner as doing so can be uncomfortable. This leads to a potential lack of communication, and communication is incredibly important in relationships of all kinds. Dealing with awkwardness is worth the reward of having a stronger connection and healthier relationship. If we don't, then the rewards within the relationship will be less; most likely, the connection will be jeopardized.

As we can see, in various areas of life, doing what is easy typically results in little reward, but if we do what is hard, we reap better rewards. And here we have it: a balance takes place, one in which our results match how much effort we put in and how much difficulty we overcome. Once again, Sir Isaac Newton's Third Law says that every action has an equal and opposite reaction, and we see that play out here: do what is easy, and one's life will be hard; do what is more difficult, and one's life will be easy. Every move we make in life has a result, so be willing to put in the effort! Only then will we achieve what we seek.

Now that we understand this about life, let's look at what happens as we go through the process of getting that reward.

🗺 *Navigation Knowledge*

Life is all about giving to get, and what we give—i.e., our effort—plays a big role in our reward. If we are willing to go through the difficulties of making something work, the reward will be grand. If we choose to do less—i.e., if we do what is easy—life will match that effort with an equal and lesser reward.

Stages of Achieving (the Obstacle Course)

Being aware of how things work and what has a high probability of working can give us an edge in life. It can help a person remain in stance towards achieving a certain result in life, which is the reason I am sharing this. This is something I learned and personally went through during an experience in 2017. Now everyone is built different so the stages may make or break a person, though I can say that it's just mind over matter. Having an understanding of these stages will feed the mind all the way to the finish line.

A week or so following the September 10th, 2017 hurricane that hit Florida, I discovered that a palm tree in my backyard had been damaged. The tree had originally been 12 to 15 feet tall, but the winds from the storm had snapped off the top of it. At the time, I was unfortunately in the process of listing my house for sale, so after the storm hit, I needed to clean the property up a bit to make it more presentable to potential buyers.

Now, what I'm about to say might sound crazy to some, but if you're also a person who is fueled by knowledge and growth, you might see why I did what I did: I decided to remove the palm tree with my bare hands as a sort of test. I decided to treat it like a goal I would work toward. Could I do it? (After all, I thrive on challenges.) And how many hurdles would I be met with during this process? I had always heard that "He who says he can and he who says he can't are both usually right." Would I be able to keep an "I can do it" mindset?

So I set up my camera to record this experiment. The first try was easy because my mind hadn't yet been hit with resistance—at the start, the thought of trying to rip down the tree with my bare hands seemed fun. I can't recall feeling any difficulty during the first four tries as I was still carrying a strong belief that I could do it. When round 5 came around, I started to adjust my tactics to try and get a better result. After I adjusted and approached round 6, well...by then, I was recognizing the true difficulty of my endeavor, so I was starting to lose a bit of the belief and confidence I once had.

Unfortunately, my new approach didn't really shift things for me. The next round started to make me a bit tired, but I was still able to just push through. I was starting to go through the stages that lead to achievement, toward reaching my goal. But by the eighth round, frustration set in, and I could tell that I had gone from having a strong belief to having a not-so-strong belief. I could see how many people might have just given up at that point, but because it was an experiment and I was recording it, I knew I definitely wouldn't feel good about giving up.

Round 9 came and went, and I had my first negative thought. Right after that, I started noticing that I was doubting myself big-time. Once again, though, I kept trying, overriding the negative thoughts as much as possible and push through. A few more rounds, and I was experiencing physical pain—I had tingling in my arms and was bleeding from cuts on my hands. I was really doubting I could achieve the result I wanted; my confidence was getting pretty low. I was exhausted, it was getting dark, and my phone battery was about to die. I felt more and more like giving up. Before that could happen, though, I told myself I'd try one more-round (which I was now approaching the fifteenth).

I tried and tried and tried. Nothing. The palm tree was not coming down. I stopped for a second and wondered if I had more left in the tank. I was lightheaded and dizzy, but there I went, I continued to pull and push on the tree. Still nothing. I had almost no energy left. It was round 17. Negative thoughts had taken over my mind; I was pretty much convinced I couldn't do it. But I recognized what I was going through and took control of my thoughts. I told myself that I needed to find a way to continue.

It was round 18, and I was extremely burnt out. I was having more negative thoughts, like *No one's around to see if I quit. But that's not who I am. What the heck—let's go again.*

Nothing. The tree just kept bending and wouldn't uproot. I was done—I had given it 18 rounds of effort and my phone was about to shut off and it was almost dark out. I was feeling beat-up and heart was racing tremendously.

But no! I have to override this negative, defeated mindset and give it one last try! I thought. *I can do this! It will come down!*

Round 19. I ran full-speed at the tree, and with my last tiny bit of energy, I jumped and grabbed the highest point and pulled down with all my weight. As I did that, my feet landed on the ground with the tree trunk still in my hands, but this time I felt it give a little. A lightbulb went on in my mind, and I started aggressively pulling down harder. I felt I had this thing now! I was not stopping, because I could sense the finish line was near.

BOOM!! The tree started to make crackling sounds. I hadn't uprooted it—I had snapped it off. An amazing feeling of accomplishment ran through me. I pulled and tugged the trunk off and then ended up lifting it up over my head as I achieved my victory. A once-tired me all of a sudden felt energized and accomplished.

I'll tell you what: that day, I learned something new. I learned that in order to achieve our goals, we must go through many stages to get our reward, and the reward will match the effort. The more effort and difficulty we have to go through and the bigger the goal is, the greater the reward will be. If you're trying to accomplish something big, expect insane resistance, because the end result will be a very valuable one. A smaller or even medium-sized goal won't be as difficult, but still, the path and direction is the same—one just has more obstacles than the other does.

Below is a visual representation of what it takes to succeed at a goal.

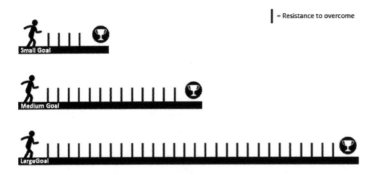

If we're aware of the potential challenges ahead of time, I think having this insight will help us not give up so easily—it will be easier for us to have faith to push through when we know what to expect. Too many people give up much too soon. On average, lots of us only make it through the first few stages of the difficult obstacle course that lies between our current reality and achieving our future goals. Once doubt starts to set in, it's very tough to convince ourselves that we should go on. But if we are aware that these challenges are supposed to happen, then our mind can overcome them more easily. Next time one is met with resistance for a goal of theirs, think about that tree and me. If you persevere and respond the same, you can expect the result to be the same: success.

Navigation Knowledge

If you're aware of the stages you'll need to go through to achieve a goal, then there's a good chance you'll keep trying and therefore eventually achieve success. Whether a goal is small, medium, or large, the direction is the same—some goals just take a bit longer to achieve than others.

Time Management

I was in my thirties before I started to consider what time is and really pay attention to it. Now, I look at time as movement, direction, space, evolution, change, and growth. Once I started looking at time a little deeper, I started to look at the world and what's been accomplished so far. When I did that, I saw two differences: things created by humans, and things not created by humans. The things that were not created by humans, like animals and trees, seem to go in a certain direction with time. Usually that's a positive direction, like growing or getting smarter/bigger or reproducing. This seems to be a goal for the world, the direction it wants to go in: a positive direction of growth, power, and energy.

So as a human I've started to look at my life in the same way. The direction I should be going in—the one it seems the world wants me to go in—growth. And since I have been given this opportunity and time here on earth to grow, how should I do that? Well, let's first look at how the majority of us are choosing to use time today and what we as a whole have conformed to doing.

As I've mentioned earlier, many of us seem to be playing the "Follow the Follower" game here on earth. We are born, we become a byproduct of our environment, we go to school, we get a degree, we (hopefully) save money, we (hopefully) find a partner, we get a job, we get married, and then we have kids. Lots of these things are great to do, but here we are talking time management. The majority of us have all of that wrapped up and done in our twenties. Unfortunately, shortly after that, our lives just become a daily repetitive cycle of doing pretty much the same thing.

What happens next? Well often, we get bored—we know we have lots of time still left to live. Many people eventually start-wishing for more; at that point, and they either do something about it or just accept their situation (since it's often easier to just not think about it). However, one will naturally start to yearn for more from life, and that will start to surface as little hints. Such as one making comments like, "I wish I knew then what I know now."

I know I've heard not only that last comment, but even things like, "Chris take your time getting married—you have plenty of time." "Chris, go travel! Do it before you have kids." Usually, people who say that are older, and my takeaway from those sentiments is that they didn't use their time wisely—it's obvious that the majority of them wish they could go back and play things differently.

That last sentence is the key here: *they wish they could go back and play things differently.* I think it's wise to think carefully about how one is going to play their cards with the time they have on this earth. If we do, we'll be more likely to achieve the life we truly want. We'll be able to navigate life better. Which is why I'm kicking out this information trying to reach those early.

Everyone should be living the good life we dream about. Doing so is truly not far-fetched at all—it only seems difficult because we never received the proper programming early on, and that has limited our odds of achieving success. The life we want appears impossible. But it's not, I promise you! In order to achieve it, we just need to focus on the four pillars *and* on how to use the time we're given.

That said, I need to focus on one particular pillar for a minute, because it's one that many of us spend our whole lives chasing and, in the process, disrupt our chances to really make big gains in other areas. I have been guilty of spending too much time on this pillar myself. Yes, I'm talking about the love & relationships pillar again. I was focusing on that as my main target because of the good feelings it brought me. But here's the thing—I needed to relax and understand that love isn't going anywhere. As long as we all don't become completely numb, it won't go away any time soon. (This may be a bold projection on my part.)

What do I mean by that? Well majority us seem to always want to focus on that love pillar, from our youth to our older years. In fact, most of us run around frantically trying to find the love of our life, to the point that our overall life becomes a bunch of highs and lows while our wealth and health pillars are most likely being neglected. The reason I say "highs and lows" is because most of us go through various heartbreaks in our life.

How can we deal better with that? Well, I believe love isn't going anywhere, so I focus my time on the health and wealth pillars. This allows me to not only showcase the best of myself (which will help me when I do meet my future partner), but it also allows me the chance to create a life rich with meaning, a life with fewer limits and financial troubles. This approach of playing life in order of what's important strikes me as a winning situation, whereas playing it the other way and putting all of my attention on the love pillar seems like putting the cart before the horse.

Once people graduate from college, many of them go right into having kids, getting married, and buying a home. To me, this seems like skipping several stages of growth and not utilizing the wealth pillar to its fullest extent. It would be wise to be more patient with these things, especially when we're still in our twenties. Maybe it would be better to focus on attaining great health first, for example, and then focus on the wealth pillar. Unfortunately, most people don't see that path—they see what everyone else is doing and think that that must be the best way. Those who play life differently are viewed as being odd. "Why don't you settle down?" Is something they might hear. I know I have plenty of times.

Personally, I don't feel the standard approach brings the best results, so I'm playing my cards differently. I'm learning from myself and I'm learning from others as well. I think it's best to live a life wherein income outperforms debt rather than live a life that involves creating multiple expenses and then trying to figure out how to generate income to survive those debts. That kind of life generally means living paycheck to paycheck, and it's what happens when we don't focus more on understanding the wealth pillar from the beginning. Most people just get a job to have money to get by—they hope to figure out their finances later. That "later" comes and goes...and now they have kids, so they don't have much time to work on their wealth pillar. Plus taking risk becomes much less, due to having kids. Add the expense of a home to the mix, and one's liquidity options and ability to invest are limited.

For many people, that scenario unfolds in their twenties and early thirties; now they're unfortunately stuck trying to maintain their belongings, becoming a slave to their car payments and house payments. They go to a 9-to-5 job that they don't like. They live for the weekends. (I know this from personal experience) They think maybe when their kids go off to college, they will travel more etc.

On top of all that, there might be tension in their relationship, in large part because their finances are tight— its common today that a lot of couple's divorce over financial stresses. They also might have evolved and changed since their younger days and are maybe growing apart. If both partners were just a little more patient and hadn't fast-forwarded through so many life decisions during that time, they might find themselves in a different position, possibly *not* one where they're stuck in a routine and feel like they didn't really get to do what they wanted to do in life. I hear a lot of people voice these kinds of regrets aloud, saying things like, "Chris, you are so lucky that you don't have kids and get to travel" or "I wish I had time and money so that I could do some of the things I see you doing."

I'm so glad I listened to those before me who passed along insightful and helpful guidance. The truth is that I *do* want kids, and I can still have them—I've just decided to play my cards differently. I'm not saying this to praise myself, but to encourage others to think about the time they have in life and utilize it wisely. I'd like everyone to be able to navigate this game of life better.

At this moment, I can choose to settle down by finding a partner in life and soon have kids. As I've stated, love isn't going anywhere it's in high demand of the masses. So the difference in my life between myself and others is the following. My heath and wealth pillars got more attention early on, and now I feel great, am less likely to suffer from disease, and feel confident about the way I look. I'm in a good financial position, one that gives me a higher chance of having the house I really want or the cars I want for myself and my eventual wife. My kids would get more financial support and more time from me because I've learned how to *create* a job rather than just *get* a job. I've learned how to invest my money, which really helps with obtaining financial freedom. I don't just live for the weekend—every day is amazing and has fewer limitations. Anyone can accomplish these things if they manage their time wisely while also giving the pillars proper order and attention.

If we stop and look at how much time we actually spend "living" in the current system, we'd most likely find out that we only "live" the way we want to a few hours per week. Between sleeping and working, how much time do we actually spend awake and doing what we want to do? Our time is valuable; this thing called life isn't forever, at least not here on earth. Something I learned from Gary Keller's book *The One Thing* was to use time blocks to manage my time each day. Whenever I am working on something very important, I dedicate time each day of the week to spend doing my "one thing" that I'm trying to bring to life. I know distractions will come my way, so I must protect that time.

Below is visual example of what I sometimes do.

	Meal	Gym	Work w/Meal	Meal	Break	Time Blocked Goal	Sleep
Mon	7:30 - 7:55	8:00 - 8:45	9:00 - 8:00	8:15 - 8:30	8:35 - 9:30	9:35 - 11:30	12:00 - 7:00
Tues	7:30 - 7:55	8:00 - 8:45	9:00 - 8:00	8:15 - 8:30	8:35 - 9:30	9:35 - 11:30	12:00 - 7:00
Wed	7:30 - 7:55	8:00 - 8:45	9:00 - 8:00	8:15 - 8:30	8:35 - 9:30	9:35 - 11:30	12:00 - 7:00
Thurs	7:30 - 7:55	8:00 - 8:45	9:00 - 8:00	8:15 - 8:30	8:35 - 9:30	9:35 - 11:30	12:00 - 7:00
Fri	7:30 - 7:55	8:00 - 8:45	9:00 - 8:00	8:15 - 8:30	8:35 - 9:30	9:35 - 11:30	12:00 - 7:00
Sat	7:30 - 7:55	8:00 - 8:45	9:00 - 8:00	8:15 - 8:30	8:35 - 9:30	9:35 - 11:30	12:00 - 7:00
Sun	A day for myself						

In terms of how I use my day-to-day time, you won't find me constantly straightening things up, mowing the lawn, or worrying about my car being clean all the time. These ongoing things in life can distract us from the bigger picture and interrupt our focus. Little tasks can easily add up and eat up our time when that time can be better used elsewhere, perhaps to pursue a goal that could really shift ones life. When I was younger, my mentor John would always ask me why I still mowed my own lawn. He finally got through to me that I needed to hire someone to mow the lawn and then use that time to pursue my goals instead.

It's easy to get sucked in and constantly give a lot of time to these ongoing maintenances of life...but if you do, you'll spend less time focusing on your goals, which won't benefit you in the long run. If you focus on your goals, though, and also make it a point to balance all of the pillars, you'll be successful. Maybe having things tidy is at the very top for someone, which is fine as we're all built different. However, for those who like myself view these ongoing maintenances as secondary to their main objective. Then putting their goals over these small maintenances of life and neglecting them from time to time gives them the edge of improving their bigger picture. They know what's more important because the impact it can bring. I know at any time I can clean my home, my car and quickly bring it up to speed. In my heart I can achieve both results but one needs to be ahead of the other due to its difficulty. It's like looking at the easy goals verse hard goals section, with the hurdles in front of them. I'm aware they're easy but also offer less satisfaction for me so I don't place them high in my rankings. Plus me neglecting them at times is just temporary.

The last thing I'll share is what I noticed not too long ago. The same order as the health, wealth, love, and fulfillment pillars is actually how my days unfold. I wake up and usually go to the gym in the morning. I then focus on generating wealth afterwards, by the evening I might spend time with that special someone or friends of mine. This has been my approach in life lately and has worked well for me. So please feel free to adopt this in your life as well, I'm sure it will help bring success and balance as it has for me.

Navigation Knowledge

How we utilize our time early on in life can really affect our position later in life. When we recognize how important the wealth pillar is and give it our proper attention, we'll have more successful and balanced lives. Remember, it's wise to place the horse and cart in proper order, and not the opposite. Make sure one increases their income before they accrue more debt.

Distractions

Boy, do we all get caught up in distractions from time to time. Not to mention procrastinations. It's okay to take a break from one's path and mission to dive into something of interest—having those moments when we step away from what we are pursuing in life helps us recharge. The only time stepping away hurts us is if getting distracted starts turning into a routine and pulls us away from our important goals. At that point, distractions become a real problem. But being aware of what our distractions are gives us an upper hand and is a huge advantage when it comes to navigating life successfully. We need to recognize when we're distracted and not let that become our norm.

One of the biggest distractions today is...wait for it...you know what it is...the mobile device! We've gotten sucked into our phones and really have a hard time staying away from them. The next distraction (which will be much worse) is going to be virtual reality in my opinion. Then we'll actually be even more inside the device.

Unfortunately, many of us can agree today that there will always be events that happen in this world. Once one is slowly dwindling out, another resurfaces to replace it and then grabs the world's attention yet again. The reason I'm mentioning it and where it becomes a problem, is I see people waste a lot of energy and time getting distracted—caught in this cycle eating away at their time, pulling them away from their problems and pursuits like a time burglar. We need to start recognizing what's happening so that we can redirect our attention and energy toward what will help us prosper in life. Many portals to these distractions in the world work most of the time to generate money and ratings but we won't dive into that here. However, the media does have such great power to take anything in the world, broadcast it, to get an emotion out of the humans. Once that happens it steals the time and joy from the those taking it in depending on what it is. What happens from that moment can cause one to feel unpleasant. Their natural reaction becomes projecting what we feel onto others at work or even onto more social media channels. The reason for this response is they didn't like what they absorbed and are responding in such way to make themselves feel better. And as we know all humans are striving on a day to day basis, to feel good. It's wise to recognize and not fall victim to this all-too-common scenario that is happening right now for many.

I've observed thousands of people sharing their feelings via social media on whatever latest topic is trending. It's a complete distraction and sucks them into something that is so trivial in the grand scheme of their own lives. Many people waste countless hours typing away, trying to get an opposing party to agree with them and vice versa. It's a vicious cycle and a huge distraction. So many giving another and mostly a stranger on the internet their time and attention which very is counter-productive. If we're worrying so much about other people's lives, then we are probably neglecting and failing at our own. That's just one of the many distractions that can get in our way as one is trying to achieve the good life.

If we pay close attention to social media, we'll notice the two personalities illustrated below: the talker who constantly chirps away and the critic who lurks and picks at what the talker says. Most people have become one of the two. I recommend steering clear of those interactions, especially early on in life and being that third personality: the doer. That's the one many people wish to become or think they already are. The doer is busy making things happen and knows that just talking or criticizing gets nothing done and is a big distraction. There's no question here of who will get the fruits of life—the doer will.

Another distraction which can be very enjoyable but needs to be kept under control is going out to local hot spots with friends. It's fun and is part of the fulfillment pillar (and also possibly the relationships pillar), but going out for drinks can become more of a focus than making ideas and goals come to fruition. I've been guilty of this myself.

Distractions are only a problem when they become habits, when we spend too much time each day living in the moment and pushing worries aside. This eventually catches up to us because life will demand balance. One way I handle my craving for fun times is to book trips with my friends months in advance. That way, I can stay focused and not feel the need to go out every week, which can easily interrupt my productivity. By setting up a trip in advance, my body knows it will have a chance to recharge and that the balance I need is not a long time away.

Sometimes, though, I feel like I'm slacking off when I use my time to go have fun. I see this as a good reaction, because I establish passionate goals for myself and am very serious about achieving them. They hold a special meaning and place in my heart. It's okay to feel uneasy when you feel like you might be missing an opportunity. That "feeling disconnected" response is validation that you're on your right path in life, one that's fueled by your passion.

This reminds me of a statement I once heard from Arnold Schwarzenegger: he said that one should always remember there's someone out there right now working just as hard as you are, and when you are out horsing around, they are getting ahead. Now, that might sound like a bit much for some as we're all built different, but those words do offer great motivation for people who have ideas they want to come to fruition. Easing off the gas could result in a missed opportunity.

When I look at my own situation, I know that I like to create, and as a creator, I don't want one of my creations to be created by someone else because I was spending my time elsewhere. Consequently, I steer clear of choosing drinking with friends and playing around on social media over something that holds more meaning. And as you may know, going out partying or playing around on social media is going to be there, or if not something better that replaces it. But my time and energy I have at this point in my life is ticking away and the truth is later in life I'll have less of both. So, I discipline myself and am aware of distractions and don't get caught up in them—I don't want distractions to push my dreams aside. This is very important and the greats learned to do this. Many times, friends asked me to go here or there, maybe it was jet skiing or to go out one night. I've have turn it down repeatedly because there was something more important I was working on and what was on offer felt like a distraction at the time. I recall a time when I was writing the book "I'm thinking about getting into real estate" or some software I was developing. When I'm really engaged in a project and don't want to stop, I decline invitations to go out with friends. I love my friends, and they know I'm available if they really need me. But this is my life, and as much as it's good to spend time with friends, I can't forget the person in the mirror. That person gets neglected far too much and winds up unbalanced if we're always taking care of others. (But giving is great) Acts of service to others can go much further when you have given to yourself first. Remember, no one can pour from an empty cup!

This section is just a few examples of many things that can be a distraction as television, other peoples drama, video games, and even substance abuse can distract a person.
If one has dreams, it's that person's job to protect those dreams and not worry about things that can distract them from making those dreams become reality.

Navigation Knowledge

One of the hardest things to do is avoid the distractions that surround us. It's so easy to get sucked into allowing things to steal our time. That said, taking a break from our goals is okay—we just can't let distractions become habits that interrupt our dreams.

You Put Yourself There

When we've learned how to give up complaining and instead begin holding ourselves accountable, we'll get to the next level. Here's a statement worth remembering: "You are where you are because you put yourself there."

Many of us might not have had a great starting point in life, but that's not why our end results are poor—that can just become an excuse we give ourselves. Everyone has the ability to do great things, and each and every decision we make is ours to make. Still, many people want to point fingers and blame others for their problems and lack of success in life. "It's not my fault," they say. That mindset creates a poisonous downward cycle, one where no growth will ever take place. How can someone grow and improve if they think they never are the problem, that they always right and never wrong?

I used to be that person—I would argue and argue and paint a picture of why I was right and you were wrong. If something went wrong, it was always because the other person had messed it up, not me. Since then, one of the most powerful things I've done for myself was learn to give up complaining and blaming others. And boy, does that feel good. I have taken 100% responsibility for my own life, and I know that if it doesn't pan out, well, it's all on me.

Now I have the ability to find solutions to my problems instead of just putting them on others (which solves nothing). I've learned to never rely on someone else to make my life better or blame them for things going wrong. I am where I am now in life because I put myself here. Life is eventful, and I've learned to respond to those events with thoughtful decisions. It's all about responding properly to life.

Of course, tough times are part of life. I began to view negative times like a little test, a test that is given to mold us into greatness. Often, when we're feeling pressured and rattled, we project negative energy to others, but the wise thing to do is to control our emotions and ask ourselves a simple question: "How can I solve this problem I'm experiencing?" Rather than complaining and blaming, start thinking about how to fix it.

Let's say one of my businesses doesn't do well. A non-experienced business owner might blame the employees for not doing their job, but I always look deeper than that and ask myself, "Did I hire the wrong people? Is my training not good enough?" Whoever is running the business is the one calling the shots, so if the business fails, that's not the fault of others, it's the fault of the business owner.

Another thing to remember is that most of the time, the things that happen in life are only as big as you make them out to be. More often than not, they are trivial, but in the moment when they happen, emotions are involved, and the events seem to hold much more meaning. But truly, everything in life is temporary, even how we feel. Our emotions fade; things will pass in a day or two. Later, we'll feel differently about the situation because it will feel less intense.

In an attempt to be bothered less by emotional situations, I've adopted a new mindset: I figured out what the top five most important things in my life are, and when negative times hit, I quickly catch myself and think, *Does what I'm upset about have anything to do with the most important things in my life?* The majority of the time it's nowhere close—it's so trivial, yet in the heat of the moment, I've made it into a big deal. In that case, the rule I've made for myself goes into effect, which is, "It's not allowed to rent space in my brain."

If it's not in your top list of meaningful things in your life, it cannot rent space in your brain. In other words, you're not allowed to dwell on it—you just have to let it go. Once you make that a rule to live by, I promise you'll start having more control of your life and not react to life poorly with complaints and blaming. You'll recognize and handle the small stuff very well in life that really isn't that important. This way of responding to life will help you maintain positive energy and project positive vibes, which then causes you to become a magnet to the world. Your value as a person will be increased by operating in such way.

This kind of tweaking is a form of holding oneself accountable, as we are responsible for our reactions to negative situations and are capable of finding solutions. Others may still be operating in a way where their results just aren't as good as they like due to how they respond. If one pays attention, they will see its clear that throwing out negativity will come right back to them. This enlightened response filters the negativity and with the law of balance at play it will reward a person for creating a more positive response.

We have the option to upgrade ourselves and hold ourselves accountable for the way we respond to things; one can adopt a more advanced response that entails thinking about and recognizing emotions and reacting wisely. I will provide a bit more on this in the "Responding to tough times and negativity" section as these two parts of the book are related.

There becomes a high probability it's quite likely that your life will dramatically improve in accordance with how you respond to life's challenges. In short, you'll be more capable of achieving the good life. All you have to do is start changing your mindset and doing away with unsuccessful habits.

Navigation Knowledge

Understand that where you are in life is because of the decisions you have made so far. Learning to accept this is what teaches us to hold ourselves accountable. Being able to give up complaining and blaming can be very tough, but if you just stop and think about it, the way we respond to life is what's giving us our results. It's all on us.

Offense or Defense in Life

I once had an old friend of mine comment on a video that I had made for one of my social media accounts. The topic was how to save money. Apparently, he didn't agree with my message, because his comment about the video wasn't a very positive one. However, I didn't let that bother me, because I know that many people in the world see things differently. It's possible you might also not agree with me, either, but please hear me out.

One may have noticed by either observing others or just thinking that individuals are playing life more so on offense or more so on defense. Sometimes, people flip between the two, but most of the time, the way they approach life is mostly one or the other. Now I like to say that there are two types of people in this world: those who focus on saving money (playing defense) and those who focus on making money (playing offense). Now I want to stop for a second and give a great example I think that should help one see why I choose to play offense in life.

On February 6th of 2017, two American football teams—the Atlanta Falcons and New England Patriots—faced each other, with each team hoping to become the Super Bowl champion. Many people watched the game; plenty of people know the end result. Still, though, I want to review a pivotal moment that happened during the game. It was the third quarter, and there were 8 minutes and 32 seconds left to play. The Falcons' quarterback Matt Ryan threw a short pass out to the right to Tevin Coleman, who then ran in for a touchdown. That put the Atlanta Falcons up by 25 points. Everyone was sure the game was over—there wasn't much time left on the clock, and the Falcons were clearly dominating the Patriots. For the Patriots to win, they would have to score at least four times *and* shut the Falcons out of scoring at all. Oh, and they also had to do that in just a quarter and a half. (In case you're not familiar with football, well, that's an extremely hard task and a very improbable one.)

The Falcons would almost have to give up and make tons of mistakes on both their offense and defense...or maybe just the majority of their team would need to have a particular mindset? A mindset that I feel was on defense after they got way ahead of the Patriots. Shortly after the Falcons scored that last touchdown and went up by 25 points, Tom Brady and the Patriots marched down the field and finally scored their first touchdown. I was pretty sure I knew what the Falcons were thinking at that point: "Do not lose, do not lose! Do not make mistakes!"

But the focus on not losing <u>was not</u> what they had been focusing on throughout the entire first half—that thought had almost certainly been, "Win, win, win, win! It's ours! This Super Bowl is ours!" Well, the Falcons momentum definitely shifted to the Patriots side. The Patriots continued focusing on winning and were able to rally from a 25-point deficit (with only a quarter and a half to go) to tie the game. That led it into overtime, where the Patriots won the coin toss to receive. Then they put together a game-winning touchdown drive and were able to pull off the win as the Super Bowl Champions once again! Unbelievable!

Now you might see where I'm going with this "offense vs. defense" mindset change. Many of us were taught to save their money. Rarely do you hear people say, "Take massive risks and invest as much as you can!" or "Always go after your dreams in life!" Now there may be a selected few who received the latter advice, but it's uncommon. It's usually, "Take the safe approach and save your money."

Yes, it's good to save a bit of money, but saving money should not be the main goal and main focus in life. Why? Well, because that's a mindset driven by fear. The reason we are so focused on saving is because deep down, we fear we can't make money again—after all, it took us years to have what we have. But we only think that because we've been programmed by others who were themselves driven by fear and disbelief, who didn't go after their dreams and instead took the safe approach in life. They chose to live a limiting life, doing a job that wasn't what they dreamed of doing but was enough because it made them feel secure and safe. They hoped that one day they could retire or maybe hit the lottery so that then they could live the life they really wanted to live.

While going through life especially early on, no shots were taken at their dreams, they didn't believe in what they had in mind was possible. They have been so conditioned to think it's too much of a task, and were too afraid to even face adversity due to failure being the result. But if they stood back and analyzed themselves which many might end up doing later on. The real failure is not even trying at all, not even swinging the bat. The failure is settling for a limiting life that's just average. We may forget that time is something we cannot just create for ourselves, at least no one's figured that out yet. I'm against limiting ourselves especially early in life when I'm suggesting to instead swing for the fences and not let opportunities pass us by. Look how I have the pillars in order, before one settle's down I recommend risking as much as they can for that big pop in life and which has a chance to really shift a person's financial situation. The truth is one will not end up under bridge as long as they make positive effort in life. Now it might get extremely tough, but they will learn so much from their experience either way which helps them later in life. We gain so much powerful knowledge! We must not let failure deter us—failure means growth and the opportunity to acquire more information that makes us more intelligent.

No one knows how long each of us will be here—we might avoid rewarding risks and save for a day that never comes. And looking to retire when you're older might not result in the same highs from things that you might have gotten when you were younger. Since that's the way I think, one of my goals is to have zero money when I die. I'll leave no stocks or investments unused, especially knowing that I can use such things to positively impact the world before I depart. Why limit one's life for a day that may never come? Why have your money outlive you?

The answer, of course, is that early fear-based programming. We view money as our #1 priority, and it starts to rule us; eventually, we become slaves to it. Money outlives us because we put it on the top pedestal. I just wanted to shine some more light on this topic because I feel that most people don't really think about it. When we put on our thinking caps and play out how things might be in the future, we can learn a lot. To me, focusing on saving over generating—all the while hoping that one day comes when we can start living the life we want—doesn't seem like the best plan. I prefer to achieve that wonderful life much sooner by playing offense and making a constant effort to generate money, especially in my younger days.

Take risks early on! Don't fear losing money—it's replenishable, but time is not. We cannot make more time for ourselves. Also keep in mind it's an education. Most go to college for a bunch of general information not even on how to operate life, yet walk out in tons of debt. At least taking risk and maybe trying that business gives a person a chance for a huge reward and self-independence job wise. One can either throw money to make something happen and or to college. Both give back knowledge, yet one gives you a chance for a reward and the other a degree for a job with possibly debt. And most likely a job hired by one that risked it early on and landed the reward of their own company.

I'm big on playing offense and trying to make things happen rather than sitting back and just hoping they'll happen. If we want to win in life, we cannot have a losing mindset—we need to have a winning mindset. Our thoughts *do* become reality! That's what the greats believe. It's how they got to where they got, and it's how everyone else can, too.

Navigation Knowledge

Life is short, and when you play offense and try to make things happen, you have better chances of reaching your dreams. We don't know how long we will be here, so limiting our lives and saving for a day that might not come may not be the wisest move. In order to make things happen in life, one must stay focused on offense.

Give it Attention

Interesting fact about the phrase "Give it attention": that was originally going to be the title of this book. I changed it because there was so much more I wanted to share about life than this one main secret I that discovered.

As you may recall from prior chapters, I'm someone who operates life while understanding there are laws at play that govern us, especially the Law of Attraction and the Law of Balance. When we are giving things attention in life, we are taking ACTION and we are utilizing those universal laws. Now, I don't expect everyone reading this to be an instant believer in those principles—that's something we all need to research for ourselves. I'm big on everyone creating beliefs for themselves through their personal experiences and research. Unfortunately, most of our beliefs are based on what others have told us and not our own discoveries, but when we really start thinking about things, that's when we can become more enlightened.

Let's think about this "give it attention" (Taking action) belief of mine. The way it works is quite simple—if you keep trying to do something and you keep giving it attention, eventually, it will give *you* attention. The result we seek is available if we would just *not stop* giving it attention. However, that's easier said than done since we will face many mental, physical, and even emotional difficulties in life. But the "give it attention" belief gives me the mindset I need to push through difficulties to win. I want to emphasize that when I say "attention," I mean positive attention, not negative. Negative attention could really skew the results.

I'll never forget the first time I learned about the "give it attention" belief. It was in my earlier days when I first started my real estate business. I had a listing that just wouldn't sell, even though I had treated that property the same as I had treated the other properties that *did* sell. There's a system I had in place which always seemed to work, if I priced the property right and displayed a good product it would equal a sold sign. But this particular property left me baffled—I had no other ideas about what to do.

So, what did I do? Well, I decided to just give it more attention. Maybe I could take new pictures—better pictures—of the house. Maybe I could add an air freshener or two to the home so that the next potential buyers would be greeted with a fresh smell. I wouldn't do anything fancy, I'd just give the property more of my attention. The result from this approach was great. I received more traffic on the home, and *BOOM!* I got an offer.

Maybe that was a coincidence...or maybe it wasn't, but I've tested this belief multiple times since then and have always found it to be true. In fact, my mentor and business partner, John, sometimes would have moments like that and would vent to me that his sales were slow. I always responded that he knew why his sales were slow. "John," I'd say, "You haven't been giving this business attention lately because you've been focused on your other businesses. I can understand why your sales are slow."

He would nod and reply, "You're right, and I know that. I just need to give this business more attention."

Exactly! And sure enough, a few weeks would go by, and John

would be back in action, with several deals in the pipeline. We have a phrase that we say to each other all the time: That is that we both have this switch we can turn on. It's like we can walk away from the business and sales go down, come right back and boom we're generating all these sales. We hit this switch. But really, what we are doing is giving the business more attention. Remember this saying which I have mentioned prior, "where attention goes, energy flows."

Right now, you're giving yourself attention with reading this book, and that attention is returning to you by promoting growth. It's just like I talked about at the beginning of this book—with the tree that was trying to show me how growth works early in life, yet I didn't see the correlation. But that tree which was not created by us humans is a symbol of how things do work, and a positive one at that. As time goes on, we continue to mature and develop as people. How far each of us goes depends on how much effort and attention we give ourselves and our passions. As one sees, the tree doesn't get distracted, it stays ground and focused on one thing and one thing only, growth. And that growth eventually leads the tree to its purpose in life. It provides wonderful shade at times, a home for living things, oxygen for us, and even displaying such beauty. Once we start to look a little deeper at things, we open our minds and start to see life differently. But most of us are distracted at the surface level, and our attention is being pulled away from ourselves and onto other things. Our own lives seem to be put on the backburner as we're occupied elsewhere, most likely on a digital screen (which has most definitely stolen humanity's collective attention).

Now, I've realized that every mind does judge a person

naturally from time to time whether positive or negative. But with that aside I want you to think of someone you know who appears to struggle with health or financial issues. Ask yourself, what caused them to be in such a situation? Were they giving the health and wealth pillars enough attention, or had they kind of given up on them? Let's even go a bit deeper. Do you feel they guided improperly early in life? Did they not receive the right support and information when it came to navigating life?

As we keep analyzing one's situation, we can usually see where things went wrong. For most of us, the true problem is that we were misguided at an early age and then fed terrible information that didn't set us up for a successful life. I don't want that to be you. I'd like you to take what I've learned so far since it has worked for me and actually use it. Taking a risk on my words would put many people way ahead of me. Obviously, I seem to speak as if I'm talking to those early in life which is because I want to hit the root and catch those early. But many of us still have time to apply what we've learned to our life to make improvements before we depart. As long as there's time left on the clock, just like those New England Patriots had, you can create your winning moment. You just have to give your life attention. If you give something attention—positive attention—it will most certainly give *you* attention. What you want to happen is available, and taking this approach will play a part in bringing it to you.

Navigation Knowledge

If we want results in a certain area of life, one just has to stick to this belief: give it attention, and it will give you attention. Yes, there may be some obstacles in the way, but we have to stick to the plan. Don't stop giving it attention until you've gotten the result you want.

Responding to Tough Times and Negativity

As I write this section of the book, I'm going through one of those tough times myself. It's not the first time and definitely won't be the last, but the way I respond to these negative events is something I had to teach myself. I used to react with anger and snap at people, but now I control my thoughts and therefore my reactions better, at least 98% of the time. (I'm not perfect, either.) This controlled response seems to have stemmed from the beliefs I have created...or maybe just my understanding of life now that I'm older. How many times do we have to experience tough times before we learn that those times are inevitable? In order to have better outcomes from those tough circumstances, we need to figure out how to respond to them better, at least the majority of time.

Of course, when things get bad, we don't feel good at all. It's normal for us to want to release our negative emotions and put them on others. But those others weren't the cause of what happened, and projecting negativity on them certainly isn't right. We probably had a good chance of fixing whatever was troubling us, yet we jumped the gun and caused others to feel bad, too.

When something bad happens, I find it's best to first stop and get our emotions under control before responding. The only time we should react impulsively to tough situations is when we're in true danger. Outside of that, we should first stop and think, *How can I fix this problem?* or we should give the situation more time to unfold so that we can learn the facts and see if the situation can resolve itself. Once we've learned to respond this way, we start to make wiser decisions, because our minds see things more rationally and we're not clouded by our emotions. Apologizing for one's mistakes is a great thing to do, too, even though many people don't. Learning to respond properly to events will lessen the need to apologize, because your decisions and actions will be precise and you won't need to apologize.

One of the best ways I have learned to respond to tough situations (criticism, rejection, negativity, etc.) is to channel my initial angry reaction into productivity. Yes, that's right! When things seem to not go in my favor, they become a great motivator for myself. Strong emotions start to erupt, and I turn them into fuel—whether it's a goal or a project, I take it all out on work. It's been such a blessing to me that I now respond to dark times this way. Consequently, I've accomplished so much. I'm fairly sure this is a new habit I have created for myself, because I wasn't always this way—I learned how to change, and then I did some reprogramming. The first time I got to respond to a problem in this more rational way gave me a great result. Now I obviously cannot expect everyone to respond instantly this way as we all will improve at our own pace. However, one can slowly develop this more rational response over time, eventually making it a habit. We can take something that could be destructive and make it productive. The next time things don't go your way or you receive criticism from others, use those negative moments and turn them into positive fuel.

Many of us fear criticism and rejection, but both need to happen to help us grow as a person. As I mentioned previously, there are talkers, critics, and doers. It's helpful to recognize that the critic is almost always someone who isn't willing to risk anything and possibly is waging an inner battle. For example, maybe your success and what you're doing is causing them to feel inferior—criticism from a stranger, family member, or friend most likely has a deeper cause and is not truly about you. Understanding this will help you respond properly and with less of an emotional reaction. In other words, you won't get rattled because you are aware of why they're behaving that way.

When you've leveled up in life in terms of being able to better respond to negative events, it's because you've learned two things: 1. How to control your emotions and have rational thoughts and 2. Although many things in life are outside of our control, how we respond to those things *is* within our control. We have the ability to control our own thoughts and own actions from negative events. However, just to point out, there are a few things in life such as who we come in contact with and even where certain thoughts stem from that are outside of our control.

I can recall many times when I have been rejected. It used to rattle me and really knock me down—I would start to obsess about my flaws or doubt my capabilities. Those rejections could be anything from a woman turning me down to not getting a job I wanted. I know I can't control how someone else feels about me or how a hiring manager views my skills. But I *can* take massive action to try to change the situation and make it better. That's what I try to do now, especially if it's something I truly want.

However, sometimes life is trying to send you in another direction, maybe one that's more toward what you need but might not yet see. In my early twenties, when I was trying to discover what career path to go down, I was met with resistance. I was being pushed in another direction; just thinking about that now is mind-blowing to me. I had no clue then that I would be doing what I am today.

Back in 2004-2005, I really wanted to get a job with a local cable company. I kept calling their HR department to follow up about being hired. After multiple attempts on my part, I finally got an answer: they did not want to hire me, at least not at that time. After that, I remember trying get any job, from electrical work to being a banker at a local credit union which so happened to deny me for failing the phone interview. So none of those worked out, but I did get a call back from a home builder company. I was also trying to get my real estate license at the time, too, although I don't think the license was required for the position.

A few days after I got the call, I was on my way to their corporate office in Florida for the interview. As I walked through the offices, I noticed a young lady whom I knew from high school. She made eye contact with me as a way of acknowledgment, but neither of us said anything as I walked by and went into the office for my interview. Instead of an in-person interview, they had me take a personality test. I did just that, and then had to wait for an email or callback to see if I passed.

Several days went by, and I finally received an email. They told me in the nicest way possible that I wasn't a fit for their company as I didn't showcase the kind of personality they were looking for. That made me feel awful, like I was such a loser and not very smart. The younger me was really concerned about how others saw and felt about me. And just thinking about the girl I knew there knowing I was no good and didn't get the job bothered me.

That was a frustrating time—I kept getting doors closed in my face, which really bummed me out. However, what I didn't know then was that sometimes doors needed to be closed in my face in order to push me in another direction. Plus, being able to deal with disappointment and learn how to respond properly meant that I had to grow as a person. Here I am later in life and know that sometimes I have to take a good look at those doors and maybe start closing some of them myself instead of waiting for life to come around and do it for me.

When doors close, it's usually a sign that life is trying to push you in another direction. Tough times usually hit for a reason. It took me a while to start accepting this. But when a home builder rejects you for being a potential salesperson for them and then you get catapulted into another direction such as being real estate agent and go on to close over $50 million in sales (yes, that's what ended up happening after those rejections), it's much easier to accept that when times are tough, life is setting you up for something better. You start to trust that things are unfolding as they should and you don't let the tough times get the best of you.

We cannot control everything...and maybe sometimes we shouldn't, because what we think is right for us isn't always right. Once more time has gone by, we can see why something happened. So, whether you are dealing with rejection, criticism, negativity, or hate, start to form new habits for yourself. Turn tough times into productive times by taking action and being of the mindset that life events are sometimes for the best. And remember, unless you're in immediate danger, never let your emotions take over—first, make sure you think about rational solutions. After having made great positive efforts, if a door closes on you, then it was meant to close. Be patient—that door closed for a reason, and that reason will soon be delivered to you.

Navigation Knowledge

Unless we find ourselves in immediate danger, we should respond to all negative events in life with controlled emotions and great thought. This allows us to respond better and pursue better outcomes. Also, trust that life sometimes closes doors on purpose. We may not always see it at the time, but later, we will understand. So have faith in life and trust it knows best.

Diplomatic for the Win

When I first understood the importance of diplomacy, I felt like it was a revelation when delivered by Dale Carnegie. I was caught off-guard and was intrigued, because I had never had anyone explain to me something that I was already doing. I had always related to this approach in life but had never understood how to explain/teach it to others. I just felt it was an art of working with people, which it is, so I tried to share with others examples to teach them as I've always wanted to pass it along—as I was getting exceptional results from both my business and my personal life thanks to being diplomatic myself. It's really what made my relationships with others fruitful and even the foundation of my real estate success.

A good friend of mine, Bryan, excels at operating in a diplomatic way, both in his business and in his personal life. I think this ability stems from understanding humans and how we are built. It's pretty much a universal approach where majority of time, no matter who a person comes into contact with, they will be receptive to what one is giving off. Now, we will not always be able to please everyone, but that should never steer one away from doing what's best. We know that we all just want to feel good, so why rub people the wrong way? Sometimes we might not know that we are; others may be aware that they are, but just don't care which isn't good. I personally want to live life to the fullest and reap the best of what life can offer, so I strive to be diplomatic for the win. Not only does that make other people's lives better, it makes *my* life better. It's all about being direct and honest in the right way. By doing so my results is what I want, good, positive and not the opposite. You see for me I want positive outcomes in life, I want my surroundings to be wonderful and amazing.

Because all in all, my body wants it, that feel good so this is why I operate in such way.

Now before I provide some examples to help you understand this approach more, I want to point out that there will be times that I drop the diplomatic me and operate in a not so diplomatic manner. This is only when a line has been crossed and it's time to handle things a bit different, however the majority of the time it's in a diplomatic way.

One of the most helpful ways to operate in such a fashion is to put yourself in someone else' shoes. To be able to find solutions in life and bring things to a positive result it is a must. Here's an example.

Let's say Bob is in the process of looking for a new home. He walks into a model home and is greeted by Dan, the sales agent. Bob has had a bad experience in the past with home-buying and obviously isn't a fan of salespeople or the sales process.

Dan starts to ask Bob simple questions such as "What are you looking for?" but Bob's responses are very short, one-word answers. As Dan continues to engage, he notices that Bob seems uneasy and is not opening up much. Instead of Dan responding in a cold manner that would match Bob's, he decides to try to put himself in Bob's shoes. In his mind, if Dan was operating in such manner like Bob, what would be the cause? He's looking to buy a home and has a sales agent trying to communicate with him. Hmm... Within a few seconds, Dan realizes that Bob might have not had a pleasant sales experience in the past, and that's causing him to act in a cold manner.

Dan decides to communicate to Bob now a little differently. He asks, "Are you a first-time home buyer?" Bob says that he's not. Dan continues with a follow-up question: "Were your past home-buying experiences good experiences?" Bob replies a bit differently now—he opens up and explains to Dan that no, it wasn't, and he doesn't really enjoy this process.

Here's where Dan takes on more of a diplomatic approach, because now he's aware of Bob's past difficulties and that he's sensitive to the home-buying process. Dan replies, "Well, we both know that I'm a salesperson and that not everyone is fond of salespeople. After all, we all have had that time where we were lied to or some fine-print suckered us into something. Where we were misled, and it was a negative experience."

When Dan says this, Bob's demeanor starts to change, as what he is hearing is eliminating his worries.

Dan continues. "So, Bob, if you choose to purchase a home through us and have something specific you want to be cautious of, I can help you double-check on those things to prevent any issues similar to your past experience."

Bob replies, "Okay, yes—that would be nice."

As Dan continues speaking to Bob, he continues to put himself in Bob's shoes and is honest with Bob, sharing his concerns and being sensitive to how Bob feels about the situation. That way, they both have a chance to achieve what they desire: Dan wants to sell a home, and Bob would like to buy one. Because Dan is operating in a diplomatic way, Bob knows that it's safe to give him a shot and that his bad past experience probably won't be repeated with Dan.

Putting yourself in someone else's shoes is what helps this be an art of dealing with others, (As shown in the example mentioned) one that can help you navigate to a result that both desire. This is such a powerful trait to possess. Being diplomatic can help one reap great results in life. Choosing your words carefully and delivering them with consideration can also shift the mood and direction. Once again, this is why learning how to be diplomatic can be very powerful. It helps you strive to the outcome that you truly want, which should ultimately be a good one. Unless of course you aren't feeling well and anger and negativity is ruling you.

So, here's an example of that.

Let's say John is a manager at a car dealership. He notices that his salesman, Larry, has been taking longer breaks than he should. As the manager, John has to speak to Larry and let him know that what he is doing is against company policy. Now, John could confront Larry by pulling him into his office and saying something like, "Larry, I saw you today once again spending 30 minutes longer on your lunch break. You know you can't be doing that. If I catch you again, I'm going to write you up! Got it?"

or

Alternatively, he could say, "Larry, I just wanted to check in and remind you that lunch breaks are only one hour long. I know sometimes we can lose track of time. I just want to be proactive to prevent any negative repercussions for you or me if you stretch your break past an hour."

Both approaches are telling the sales associate that he cannot continue taking longer lunch breaks—the difference is the delivery. If that's done poorly, ultimately, the relationship between John and Larry could become unhealthy. Now many could say that they don't care how they deliver their words, but if their employees are no longer a fan of them, expect their job to be harder. They will listen less, and if they don't perform well, you will be looked at as the problem. As I have always told my mentor who owns a few businesses, take care of your troops, and they will take care of you. There's a way to get your point across without being a jerk. We are all built differently, yes, but if you operate with a universal diplomatic approach, people who are more sensitive than others won't respond negatively. (Which could lead to malicious behavior on their part if they felt they were treated poorly.)

Understanding how humans work—and how we are all different but yet still the same—can help you be more effective. Next time you want to get a better result from a situation or life in general, first strive to be diplomatic. You will be amazed by not only how much better those around you feel toward you, but how positive in general the atmosphere feels. You will be feeling good yourself, it's all about being diplomatic for the win.

Navigation Knowledge

Learning to be diplomatic in the way you communicate helps influence others in a positive manner. Since everyone's built differently, adopting a universal diplomatic approach results in greater productivity for everyone as well as a more harmonious atmosphere overall.

Your Gift

When we navigate life in the way that I've been sharing with you, something very special can happen: and that something is discovering our own "gift." It might sound silly, but it can and does happen. Each person has a gift and is almost like a superpower he or she has discovered within themselves.

Earlier in this book, I discussed our beliefs of what's possible and that what we *think* is possible is often limited by the programming that comes from others and our environment. Unfortunately, this programming can prevent us from thinking that we have anything special within ourselves. If we're delivered information that is a safe average approach along with fear and an impossible belief. Then one thinking they are great and having a special unique gift won't ever be on their mind. We conform to societal averages and think we're no different from the next person, but the truth is that although we are similar in many ways, every individual has something special and unique they can offer the world.

Only when we strive to grow and mature will we have the potential to discover our gifts. As we grow, we progress in a positive state versus going in the opposite (i.e., negative) direction, and when we're in that positive state, we begin to vibrate at a higher frequency of ourselves. This mainly starts within the mind and then progresses to us learning more about life and how to respond properly to it.

Some of the following traits are indications that someone is developing a higher vibration:

- They become more self-aware
- They often experience synchronicity
- They don't complain often
- They are highly creative and showcase many ideas easily and often
- Patience comes easily to them
- People open up easily to them
- They feel confident in themselves and their abilities
- They forgive themselves and others easily
- Smiling and laughing comes easily to them
- They are empathetic toward the needs of others
- They are highly intuitive
- They feel as though they have found their calling in life

When one is operating at a higher frequency level, they increase their chances of being able to showcase their best abilities and skills. In turn, their gift starts to show itself. A main way a person discovers their gift is from doing something powerful that many simply don't do: life seems to be doing it for them and making decisions as the mind is just too distracted. And what I'm referring to is really something simple, it's just "thinking." The 1952 Nobel Prize winner Albert Schweitzer was once asked "What's wrong with men today?" He paused for a second and then stated, "The trouble with men today is that they simply don't think." After hearing that, I couldn't help but agree tremendously—it is so powerful to simply spend time immersed in thought.

Now that I'm older, I spend a lot of time thinking about how I can improve my life. Doing so definitely plays a vital part in my success today. On average, I'd say I spend around 5 hours every day thinking about life and my dreams. In the process, I discover so many things about myself, things that help me develop. All of the motivational videos and books I've seen and read have caused me to stop and think and then work on myself to make changes.

When I started doing this, everything shifted and sent me in a new direction. (Maybe a gift of mine is knowing how to help another person find their gift?), but I'm not sure. My research and understanding of things has allowed me to connect the dots fairly easy, at least from what I believe. Now I honestly do not know exactly what my gift is or how many one can have. Although it's possible that what I feel are my gifts may just be my natural strengths, strengths that I ultimately feel aren't that special because I think others could also possess them. Then again, maybe some of our strengths that we feel are normal *aren't* and we just don't realize that because they come to us so easily...which is probably why those strengths really are gifts. If we're unaware of them, we will keep overlooking them instead of using them to potentially improve ours and others lives. But the truth is, anyone can become aware of their gift and reach their full potential in life; anyone has the ability to separate themselves from the pack. It all boils down to what they are trying to accomplish or whether they even care to try.

Here's something I want to share, I happened to discover this in my thirties. (I'm 36 as I write this book, so my discovery wasn't too long ago.) One day, I was going through some old photos during the process of moving and selling my home. I kept thinking about my past and the person I used to be. Two photos in particular stood out: shots of me messing around with my old computer. After staring at the photos for a few minutes, I started thinking about what I was doing with my life at that time, especially given how much free time I had because I didn't have a job yet. It's clear I wasn't distracted by money or the stresses of responsibilities. Back then, I was spending my free time on the computer.

Right then and there, I learned something about myself, namely that technology was of interest to me. At the time, I was using America Online to navigate the internet. I loved AOL! As a young guy, I mostly checked out cars and motorcycles that I wanted to acquire. (Which I eventually did as I had on my vision board!) During that period of my life, I also remembered using Microsoft Paint to draw basketball and football stadiums, and I enjoyed playing a game called Rollercoaster Tycoon that allowed me to create my own theme parks and manage them just like I would a business.

I look back at that and see that I was focusing on creating traffic to the park and trying to generate revenue inside the game. Those photos sent my mind down this direction. I then started thinking about the software I had learned to use at my first job when I was starting to play around with creating graphics with Adobe Photoshop. Fast-forward almost two decades later, and I'm still using that software every week.

The reason I'm sharing this story is because it's so powerful to see what we were naturally interested in and drawn to when we were younger. There's a high probability that our interests and passions are actually disguised as our gifts, or purpose which at the very least will provide one a direction. The chances of one not giving up and quitting regarding that same interest is high as well. It's something one loves to do and would do it for free which improves such skill over and over from all the time they spent on it. That amount of time can make one an expert that showcases to others as possibly a gift. Wouldn't it have been nice if we had been taught in school how to look for that passion/gift in life and then follow it? Your passion gets your attention and eventually can lead to unlocking your gift. Most importantly, your passion had nothing to do with chasing money—you went towards it because you loved to do it.

Spending time looking back at what you loved to do will help you figure out who you really are. It helped me discover I have a passion for creating as I saw how I spent time drawing, using photoshop, building outside etc. Going back and looking at your younger self can help you also decide and what you want. As I mentioned before, you might not think your gift is a gift because it comes easily to you, but think about how many people can do that skill equally well—it's probably not too many. Choose to tap into those strengths/gifts and use what was given to you to have an extraordinary life. It's very likely that discovering your gift will lead you to your purpose and a meaningful life. You'll achieve the good life and those good feelings because you'll be feeding your soul what it wants. I can say this, I might be in my mid-thirties only, but completely aware that my knowledge now and when I'm in my fifties or sixties will be much greater. However, I'm not there yet, and my gift might not be fully mature. But I'm using this time to pass along what I know thus far, as it just seems right to try and help others live a better life at this very moment.

Navigation Knowledge

We all have a unique gift that was given to us when we were created. By looking back at our younger days, we can sometimes discover our gift, because it probably is related to what we were doing prior to all of the distractions we have in our lives now. When we focus on growing, we heighten our vibrations because we're in a more positive state. Achieving that higher level of vibrations allows us to easily showcase our gifts more so to the world.

A few of the Greats

Several years ago, I read a book called *Third Circle Theory* by Pejman Ghadimi and learned that while some people have done well for themselves and reached success, some have done that plus more—not only have they become successful, they've found deeper meaning for themselves and they operate their lives in such way that they're living out their purpose. While one might measure people by their amount of income or possessions, I feel there's a higher form of measurement, one that outdoes money and tangible items: the positive impact we can have on others, humanity. Michael Jackson is a great example of this—even after his death, he's still able to generate a positive emotion in others (i.e., have a positive impact). At every moment, it's safe to say that someone somewhere in the world is listening to his music and feeling good inside. To this day, his words and his message are still impacting the world.

Earl Nightingale, the great American author and radio speaker I've mentioned who was at the top of his field back in the 1950s, seems to have left his mark as well, as the wisdom he provided to others was making an impact then and continues to now. His work really connected with me—he opened up my mind and shined light on things I had never even thought about. (Some of what I pass along stems from his messages.) What he did while he was here on earth has impacted people in a positive way.

His words opened up my mind to see things more clearly and create a better understanding of operating life for myself. The result he is getting is tremendous as it continues to flow through me and others. By looking back, we can see that many of the greats learned from the ones who came before them. Thomas A. Scott mentored Andrew Carnegie, who later helped open the mind of Napoleon Hill, who then passed insight on to Earl Nightingale, etc. The positive impact these men have had on humanity has been a wonderful thing. When we dedicate the majority of our time to helping others live a more fulfilling life, we truly define the term "legacy."

So many greats have blessed our world! One man who has provided us with inspiration to never give up on our dreams is Michael Jordan. Once cut from his high school basketball team, years later, he went on to become the man many truly feel is the greatest basketball player ever to have played the game. He showed the world what it took to be great and achieve a dream. By demonstrating his work ethic, his ability to overcome adversity, his ability to thrive under pressure, his amazing athletic ability, his motivation and determination, and his leadership, he inspired us. He showed us what is possible and what is needed to become a great success. Yet, when he was asked what he felt his best skill was, he replied, "My best skill was that I was coachable. I was a sponge and aggressive to learn."

When you fuel your mind with effective information and knowledge, you can do pretty much anything. Michael took that information and went to work. Just a few of his many achievements are being a six-time NBA champion, a five-time NBA MVP, a six-time NBA Finals MVP, a ten-time scoring champion, the NBA Defensive player of the year, a two-time slam-dunk champion, and a two-time Olympic gold medalist.

During the time Michael was showcasing his gifts on the basketball court, another young man was making moves on

Wall Street. And "making moves" is exactly what he did—in 1994, Jeff Bezos decided to quit his Wall Street job and start an internet company. His wake-up call was finding statistics showing a 2,300% increase each year in web usage. Immediately, he started to think about what kind of business plan would work within that realm. After creating a list of 20 products he could sell on the internet, he settled on books...and those books turned into many more items, all sold through Amazon.com. Jeff created a new way for people to receive products more effectively. Not only are we getting a wide variety of products at our fingertips, we are getting fast, affordable items and are saving something we find very valuable: time. The positive impact here is helping people get what they need more efficiently and giving them more time to enjoy life. Instead of fetching the product one needs for living they can have it brought to them pretty quickly.

There are hundreds more people I could mention who have impacted the world in a positive way. Though it's not necessarily what they have uniquely done different than one another that's important here. But more so of what they did the same.

One thing the greats do is not let money dictate their path in life. Bill Gates and Steve Jobs didn't decide that they wanted to make money and so set off in a particular direction—they followed their interests, one that was so strong that in a way, their interests were written in their DNA. It was given to them and they discovered it. Once they figured out what direction they planned to set off in they took massive action going down that path.

Soon thereafter one might start unlocking their gift which is happening without them actually trying. The love and passion that is taking place will help a person overcome obstacles; the perseverance needed it is much easier to move past adversity. A person's nonstop efforts don't feel like work, it's because it's the love involved that's what gets them to the place where they want to be. Now, I'll tell you from my experience that following that path is not easy, not at all. But it is most certainly the way, and I love the journey. Following one's heart and passion will unlock one's gift.

And sometimes life will even allow us to see it take place very early on. Earl woods got to witness his child at 11 months old pick up a toy golf club and drive a ball to the center of the net. The quick discovery at this age of one finding their gift can certainly be that rare exception. Tiger Woods certainly has showcased excellence to the world from the relentless beating on his craft. It appears the greats all gave constant attention to their passion in life that soon revealed their gift. In turn they are living a life with meaning and purpose, while impacting the world.

We can either conform to mainstream society and expectations, or we can break away from them and unlock something within ourselves that's much greater. There are multiple ways up the mountain—you just have to choose your path.

Navigation Knowledge

It's clear that the greats have something in common: they didn't chase the money or anything else but their passion in life. That direction may be met with risk and difficulty, but the end result is well worth it. Chasing our passions and finding our gifts gives us a chance to live a meaningful life on our own terms while positively impacting the world along the way.

Living with a Purpose

Remember the introduction of this book and the story of the tree? The tree grew to the point where it was living its purpose. When the noise we call "distractions" is removed, one can get a better look at their life; they can get a better idea of what they should be doing here with their time. Unfortunately, not many people do that— It's completely optional to everyone but as I look around I can't help but notice that what the masses are doing, doesn't ultimately deliver what they want. I could out and I bet that if I asked random people if they are living the life they truly want, the majority of them would say, "No not really." But it's not their fault. Humanity was just never educated about themselves, about being a human.

That said, some people *have* found a better way to live life...but for many more, the paths to discovering that truth still seem to be hidden, possibly in a book on a shelf. There's nothing being given to a person that helps them make wise decisions for their future. There still seems to be a one-size-fits-all approach to life, and that approach isn't very efficient. Each of us has something to do here, a calling, but many never even discover it. The life they truly wanted to live was available, but they became complacent living in accordance with the status quo. Which then end ups with many people having regrets.

It's unfortunate, but many people *do* become more enlightened later on in life and its nice when they pass what they've discovered on to others. That's what I'm trying to do—within these pages, I know many might not really listen, but myself, well, I sure did. Those that lived longer on earth have always gave me tips on why I should do this or that in life. I then went on to research why they feel that way, or just give great thought to the life tip. And what it seems is many end up having regret because they didn't play life the way they wanted to. Once again, its not their fault entirely as the guidance early on was possibly very poor. One focused on making money, and as you now know life is much more than that. Its apart of the picture but being so one dimensional on it will create imbalances in life and can lead one to being unfulfilled. So I hope I have provided a deeper perspective on life and great ways to operate. I'm one that cares and want to help others live a better life, which may now have become part of my purpose. I think we all deserve to live better lives. We just need to step up and try to shift humanity in a more positive direction.

Thank you for taking the time to read my book. I'll end with a short walk through my mind and my story thus far which you may enjoy! I wish you an amazing life and hope that after having read my book, you may now have an even better shot at obtaining the good life.

Inside my Mind

I have shared much of my knowledge already and you probably have a good understanding of how I think and am navigating this life, but below, I've provided some additional thoughts and recaps on how I think. It's possible you may resonate with some of these ideas and not others. Either way, I want to share a little bit more about how to navigate life to get great results and live the best life you possibly can.

Fears into faith

I have turned many fears into faith, especially in the wealth department. I've said it before and I firmly believe that if I keep playing 13 black on the roulette table, I will eventually hit. During the process, I'm willing to lose many times to get my big pop in life. I'm also willing to minimize my life in order for greater things to transpire. Sometimes that means closing some doors to let new ones open. I focus on that euphoric moment happening, and I live life in that moment instead of focusing my energy on what I can lose. I've reprogrammed myself to think this way. This may appear risky to many people, but I truly think that seeing this approach as being risky comes from a place of fear.

The world wants to grow

I believe the world is trying to grow, not the opposite. If so, it could easily stop trying to produce and get its result.
In turn life would halt or reverse which would lead
to nonexistence. If the world were to halt, what would be the

point of time? Time is movement in a certain direction, and that direction is forward. Based on that belief, I try to grow, too. One way I do this is to work with and not against the universe, god, or whatever higher power you align with. This forward way of thinking has allowed me to navigate life more efficiently while producing prosperity for myself and those close to me.

Work with the laws

Yes, laws govern the earth, and not just laws that come from courts. I randomly picked up on these various universal laws and started connecting the dots. I won't go against them—I'd rather play them to my favor. It's almost like figuring out a trick in a video game that helps you navigate through it. If you find the portals in Super Mario Bros you can advance to the next stages quicker to help you reach your goal. I feel it helps me advance in life from this discovery.

Eventually I'll be gone

I am at peace with the fact that I will not live forever. As a result, I don't sweat the small stuff or complain much if at all. Yes, there are moments where I am faced with adversity and want to complain, but fortunately, such moments have been very short-lived ever since I gave up complaining and started holding myself accountable for 99% of the events in my life. Things have been much better since I made this adjustment. This is an example of leveling up as a person.

Being the lone wolf

I'm willing to stand alone if that's what it takes to excel. It might seem strange that I go to the movies alone or to a restaurant alone—I'm aware that this may not be traditionally viewed as "normal." However, I'm done with fitting in and conforming. I have to break away from the pack and do things as an individual. I love my friends and my inner circle, but I feel less stress and am more at peace when I'm by myself. It's also easier to focus on my direction that way.

Question

I question things and don't just take what's delivered to me as being "the right way." It's almost like being an anti-virus scanner on a computer—I scan the information first before I download it into my brain. For example, I removed Wi-Fi from my home and only use hardwired connections because I don't want to have electromagnetic radiation running through me at all times, especially when my body is sleeping and trying to heal. This is just one example of questioning the status quo.

Awareness

My favorite discovery, as I've analyzed all humans one day to ask myself what we are all doing. What I figured out is we are all just trying to feel good—we all have that in common. Everything we do, we do to achieve that grand result. We want money or companionship because those things provide a high. On the other hand, if our bodies are compromised and not in a state of optimal health, we might not be able to have those good feelings that we're working so hard to have. That's why health is my #1 priority. We all need to watch over our health and do what we can to improve it.

Look up a lot

If we look around and ignore everything that we humans have built, all that we'd see left is the trees, grass, dirt, water, birds, and the sky—in other words, an environment with no distractions. What would one think is going on here? How would they respond to make sense of the experience? I feel many, like myself would start looking up more noticing the sun, moon, and even the stars at night. They'd see movement and energy and start to think that somethings going on out there. In other words, that activity above would cause one to look up for their answers.

Dissecting right and wrong

We all have many decisions to make in life. My goal is to make as many right decisions as possible. I define "right" and "wrong" this way: if I've done something that caused someone else to have negative emotions, then I've done something wrong; if I've done something that caused others to have positive or neutral emotions, then I've done something right. This theory of mine works off the majority percentage of humanity, and not where a small number of people who were negatively affected as that would be the exception.

Blossom where planted

I'm aware that times will get tough and that I have to be able to continue to showcase the best of myself even during those tough times. That means I need to respond properly to negative situations and control my emotions so that I can think rationally. The playing field may not always be a good one or even a fair one, but one should always blossom as best they can wherever they're planted.

Strengths and weaknesses

We all have strengths and weaknesses, and it's good to be aware of them so that we can play to our strengths and work on our weaknesses. You can't hire someone to work out for you so that you can be physically stronger; you can't have someone go on stage and speak for you if you want to be a motivational speaker. Play to your strengths and work on your weaknesses.

Supply and demand

The value of who I can become can be determined through supply and demand: things in high supply offer lesser value, and things in low or limited supply hold much greater value. I choose to step away from the pack and go in a different direction. In turn, my chances of becoming more valuable as a person and allowing me to live an extraordinary meaningful life increase.

Not renting space in your brain

I have a rule that helps me respond to life: if something is bothering me and it has nothing to do with the top five most important things in my life, then it's not allowed to rent space in my brain. By doing this, I don't let myself hold on too many negative emotions, and I no longer sweat the small stuff in life. We only have so much time here on earth, and in the grand scheme of life, certain things just aren't that important.

My Short Story

Earlier in this book, I spoke about being cautious about who we get our information from—pay attention to what they have accomplished and experienced and what results have they received in life. Although I do not want to toot my own horn, I'd like to share more of my story with you.

I was born on Florida's east coast, in the small beach town of Melbourne. Although my family did not have great wealth to pass along, they gave me an abundant amount of support. After my parents divorced, my brother and I grew up living with our mother and stepfather in a single-wide trailer. Despite the divorce, we still remained close to our father and other extended family members. They were always present and supportive throughout my childhood years.

During my high school years, I enjoyed playing sports much more than I enjoyed academics—in fact, I struggled with schoolwork and got mostly poor grades. My teachers complained about my lack of interest and attention. When thinking about this situation today, I'd say I lacked interest and felt bored, plus I wasn't being challenged by the course work. In May of 2000, I failed to complete a half of a credit, and I was denied my high school diploma from Eau Gallie High School. Just one year later, Eau Gallie High launched a S.O.S program for students who needed to make up credits in order to graduate, so I enrolled in the program. I was joined by a few peers, one of them being my best friend, Ryan. Ryan would soon play an influential role in my academic success.

As a part of the S.O.S program, students were required to do an internship. I suffered from great anxiety, especially when it came to new or unfamiliar situations, so the very idea of an internship caused me significant stress. I struggled to land an internship position and questioned whether I would ever obtain my diploma. Fortunately, Ryan stepped in and helped me land a spot at the company where he was also interning, Wireless Dimensions. I credit this moment as being one of the biggest shifts in my life. Wireless Dimensions was a newly founded cell phone accessory business created by a 24-year old entrepreneur named John Curri. After a brief interview with John, I was hired. John would soon go on to become one of my greatest mentors.

After graduation, I completed a few college courses, but I did not remain enrolled for long. I was only 19 years old and had not discovered anything about myself that I could take pride in. Seeing young entrepreneurs in their twenties pulling up in Ferraris sparked a fire in me to become and accomplish something greater. Over the course of the next 15 years, I slowly learned about myself and what I was capable of doing. However, I experienced struggle and pain long before I experienced any kind of success.

In 2002, John sold Wireless Dimensions. The new owners kept many jobs intact, so I still held my position. However, shortly after the acquisition, I started to realize that in the corporate world, my pay was not based on my skills or how well I performed—even though I was a top sales rep at the company, I was not being compensated accordingly. Instead, others who were older, had a family, or had a college degree were paid much more despite performing at a much lower level. I realized that this hierarchy within corporate America was not going to work for me, so I started to look for success elsewhere.

Around this time, my entrepreneurial spirit kicked into gear, and I first ventured into the specialty retail business at my local mall. One month after opening my first location, I added a second location in a city just south of me. Despite my hard work and determined attitude, though, both startups were unsuccessful. However, these failures did not stop me from taking more risks. I soon jumped into the online sales world and began distributing products through Ebay. While this venture did well, it did not last long. I decided to close that chapter and begin to write the next one.

That was when I discovered my interest in real estate. However, at the same time, I began to experience multiple debilitating health problems that numerous doctors were not able to diagnose. I struggled with my health in private without showing signs of weakness or poor health to those around me. Although daily life had become difficult, I continued to pursue my real estate license through night courses I would attend after having worked long days.

In addition to my inexplicable poor health, I found myself unemployed when the company I worked for relocated to South Florida. Unable to pay my bills, I watched as my vehicle was repossessed right in front of me. My long-standing relationship with my girlfriend crumbled. I began to ask myself that one question: "Is this rock-bottom?" The main pillars of my life—my health, my wealth, and my love—had crumbled, and I was left mentally drained and exhausted. The fourth pillar didn't receive much attention at all due to how I was feeling.

The once energetic, ambitious, and determined version of myself had been knocked down by life, and knocked down hard. I attempted to pick myself up and got a job at the local Home Depot while the real estate license I had earned sat unused in the background—I needed money to pay my bills, and real estate couldn't deliver its initial earnings quickly enough. I was constantly fatigued. I describe this time in my life as practically unreal; I was living through my daily routines as if I were a zombie. But from time to time, my intense ambition and hunger would pierce through, and it was just enough to keep me progressing forward.

I decided to take a chance and reach back out to John Curri, who had coincidentally opened his own real estate firm. For the second time in my life, John gave me an opportunity to change my course. John helped me regain possession of the vehicle I had lost in exchange for working at the real estate office. A lethargic me had to push through my foggy mind to perform. There were many times that I was embarrassed about my lack of real estate knowledge and poor verbal skills compared to my colleagues, but fortunately, I was able to channel my anger and negative experiences from the previous few years into fuel to become a success within the real estate world.

Darker days became brighter, and I became more motivated than ever to succeed. I began writing down goals that I wanted to see manifest, and I changed all of my online passwords to consist of personal goals—that way, I was forced to type them daily. I focused all of my energy on my career.

A few successful years went by, but then the once-lucrative real estate market took a turn for the worse, resulting in one of the biggest real estate market crashes our generation had ever seen. While most agents were jumping out of the market, I chose to stay and keep learning. I used the time in a declining market to build a business and market myself to create value. I became very educated with respect to housing features, property taxes, and multiple listing services as well as how to write contracts and provide excellent service to clients. Being around John had its educational benefits as well—I began to observe his habits and moves within his different business ventures. John excelled at speaking, which slowly but surely advanced my verbal skills. But then, at a time when I felt I was really on the rise, my health decided to take a turn for the worse.

My symptoms flared up and knocked me out of work for over two months. I was so sick that I was bedridden and had no energy or appetite. I recall going to bed one night and thinking it was my last night on earth. No doctor in town could find a reason for my debilitating symptoms. I was suffering greatly, and no one could help me. I constantly researched ways to heal myself along with continually working with my doctors, and I discovered that my diet was the major contributor to my health problems—high levels of bacteria, fungi, and metals were burdening my body. Once I had corrected my diet, I began slowly regaining my health.

In 2009, I found a golden nugget: a recently foreclosed home on Owl Street. Its sale history made me investigate the fine-print details of foreclosure auctions. From that day forward, I kept accruing more knowledge of foreclosed properties, and I went on to help many investors purchase homes at foreclosure auctions and resell them for large profits. This all happened even during the real estate crash and declining market. Having found something I was passionate about and getting great results from it made my confidence instantly skyrocket.

My knowledge of the foreclosure industry led to a profit of a few million dollars for my investors while I reaped huge rewards myself. All the years I had spent trying to run mall and online businesses were nothing compared to the income I learned how to generate in the real estate market. As the years went by, my knowledge of real estate became more and more refined, and I was able to offer superior service to buyers and sellers as well as investors. I prided myself on never focusing on the money, but rather on helping people achieve their real estate goals by the knowledge I had acquired. I had faith the money would follow. It did.

I continued to write down my goals and watch them manifest and grow. My original goal was to sell 10 homes in a year; that slowly turned to 15, then 20, and so on. Each year, I expanded my goals, and that in turn grew my accomplishments. Finally, I was being compensated for my hard work and performance, not just because I was (or was not) part of a corporate hierarchy.

In 2016, I wrote my first book, *I'm Thinking About Getting Into Real Estate*, which is available on Amazon.com and BarnesandNoble.com. I had become a mentor to new real estate agents as well as the managing partner of a real estate brokerage firm (with John Curri). As of today, I have been involved in the sales of more than 150 flipped homes that have generated millions in profit. I have personally handled over $50 million dollars in real estate sales. Outside of that, I have been creating and innovating more, with writing projects, a line of clothing, and mobile software.

If you ask me what life is all about, I would proudly answer that life is much bigger than money—it's about the person you become after having experienced both failure and success. There will be a time when life will beat you into the ground, but you must keep moving forward. Never tap out! Follow your passion to live a meaningful life and impact the world in a positive way. While doing so, make sure you give all four pillars of your life attention: health, wealth, love, and fulfillment. Oh, and definitely look out for that gift of yours!

My approach to finding success in life has been discovered by many others as well—you will notice similarities between many quotes, laws of physics, and proverbs.

"Life truly is a boomerang. What you give, you get." – Dale Carnegie

"Life is an echo. What you send out comes back."

"What you sow, you reap. What you give, you get."

"What you see in others, exists in you." – Zig Ziglar

"Karma is the universal law of cause & effect."

"What goes around, comes around." – Proverb

If you keep giving life your attention and stimulating the law of cause and effect, you can reach the ultimate goal in life: that good feeling. You'll be living the good life because you'll become an amazing navigator of life. I do hope you enjoyed my book and it also helps you navigate life better my friends.

Please feel free to stop by my website and let me know how you're doing. I wish you great success and the life you truly want.

Much Love,

Christopher

www.ChristopherRegister.com

Made in the USA
Columbia, SC
12 March 2019